Hidden Pictures

GRADES K–1

This book has been correlated to state, national, and Canadian provincial standards. Visit *www.carsondellosa.com* to search for and view its correlations to your standards.

Credits

Editors: Carrie Fox and Kelly Warfield
Cover and Layout Design: Lori Jackson
Inside Illustrations: Lori Jackson
Cover Photo: © Jaimie Duplass

© 2009, Carson-Dellosa Publishing Company, Inc., Greensboro, North Carolina 27425. The purchase of this material entitles the buyer to reproduce worksheets and activities for classroom use only—not for commercial resale. Reproduction of these materials for an entire school or district is prohibited. No part of this book may be reproduced (except as noted above), stored in a retrieval system, or transmitted in any form or by any means (mechanically, electronically, recording, etc.) without the prior written consent of Carson-Dellosa Publishing Co., Inc.

Printed in the USA • All rights reserved.

ISBN 978-1-60418-141-8

Table of Contents

About This Book 3

Hidden Picture 1: Rectangles 4

Hidden Picture 2: Triangles 6

Hidden Picture 3: Dinosaur 8

Hidden Picture 4: Tulip 10

Hidden Picture 5: Cat 12

Hidden Picture 6: Mouse 14

Hidden Picture 7: Lamb 16

Hidden Picture 8: Bumblebee 18

Hidden Picture 9: Caterpillar 20

Hidden Picture 10: Butterfly 22

Hidden Picture 11: Doll 24

Hidden Picture 12: Dog and
    Fire Hydrant 26

Hidden Picture 13: Apple Tree 28

Hidden Picture 14: Tugboat 30

Hidden Picture 15: Crab 32

Hidden Picture 16: Whale 34

Hidden Picture 17: House and Tree 36

Hidden Picture 18: Sledder 38

Hidden Picture 19: Mittens 40

Hidden Picture 20: Groundhog 42

Hidden Picture 21:
    Valentine Hearts 44

Hidden Picture 22: Leprechaun Hat 46

Hidden Picture 23: Easter Bunny 48

Hidden Picture 24: Easter Egg 50

Hidden Picture 25:
    Jack-O'-Lantern 52

Hidden Picture 26: Bat 54

Hidden Picture 27: Turkey 56

Hidden Picture 28: Holiday Candle 58

Hidden Picture 29: Candy Cane 60

Hidden Picture 30:
    Christmas Stocking 62

Blank Graph Reproducible 64

About This Book

Early Graphing Hidden Pictures is a book of self-correcting graph paper activities designed for students in kindergarten and first grade. In each activity, students are guided to color graph paper squares one by one, causing a "hidden picture" to gradually appear. At first, you may need to work closely with students on these activities. Student independence will increase with experience.

Student Goals

- To begin left-to-right and top-to-bottom reading sequences
- To develop fine-motor skill coordination
- To employ transference
- To develop and strengthen graphing skills
- To strengthen concentration skills and attention to details
- To learn colors

Teacher Directions

1. Make a copy of the blank graph reproducible (page 64) and a directions page for each student. (Be sure to make extra copies of the blank graph reproducible because students may make errors when first learning this activity.)
2. Have students color each square on the graph paper by following the row-by-row, left-to-right information supplied on the directions page for each picture. Each student should begin with the square located at the top left corner of the blank graph paper (the first square in row A). She should color that square the color(s) indicated in the box located in the same position on the directions page. Then, each student should color the remaining squares in row A before moving on to row B, row C, etc.

Hints for Success

- Tell each student to cross out each square on the directions page when he has colored the corresponding square on his blank graph paper. Another helpful hint is to have the student fold back or cover each row of directions as he completes it.
- After each student has colored an entire graph, you may want to show her the answer key to help her add faces and other details.
- Encourage students to make their pictures more attractive by:
  a. applying colors solidly with crayons or markers and staying within the lines.
  b. blending together squares of the same color rather than outlining individual squares.

Hidden Picture 1   **Directions**

Directions: Use the information below to color each square on the separate sheet of blank graph paper.

	A	B	C	D	E	F	G
	red	red	red	red	red	red	red
	red	orange	orange	orange	orange	orange	red
	red	orange	yellow	yellow	yellow	orange	red
	red	orange	yellow	green	yellow	orange	red
	red	orange	yellow	green	yellow	orange	red
	red	orange	yellow	green	yellow	orange	red
	red	orange	yellow	yellow	yellow	orange	red
	red	orange	orange	orange	orange	orange	red
	red	red	red	red	red	red	red

Hidden Picture 1

Answer Key: Rectangles

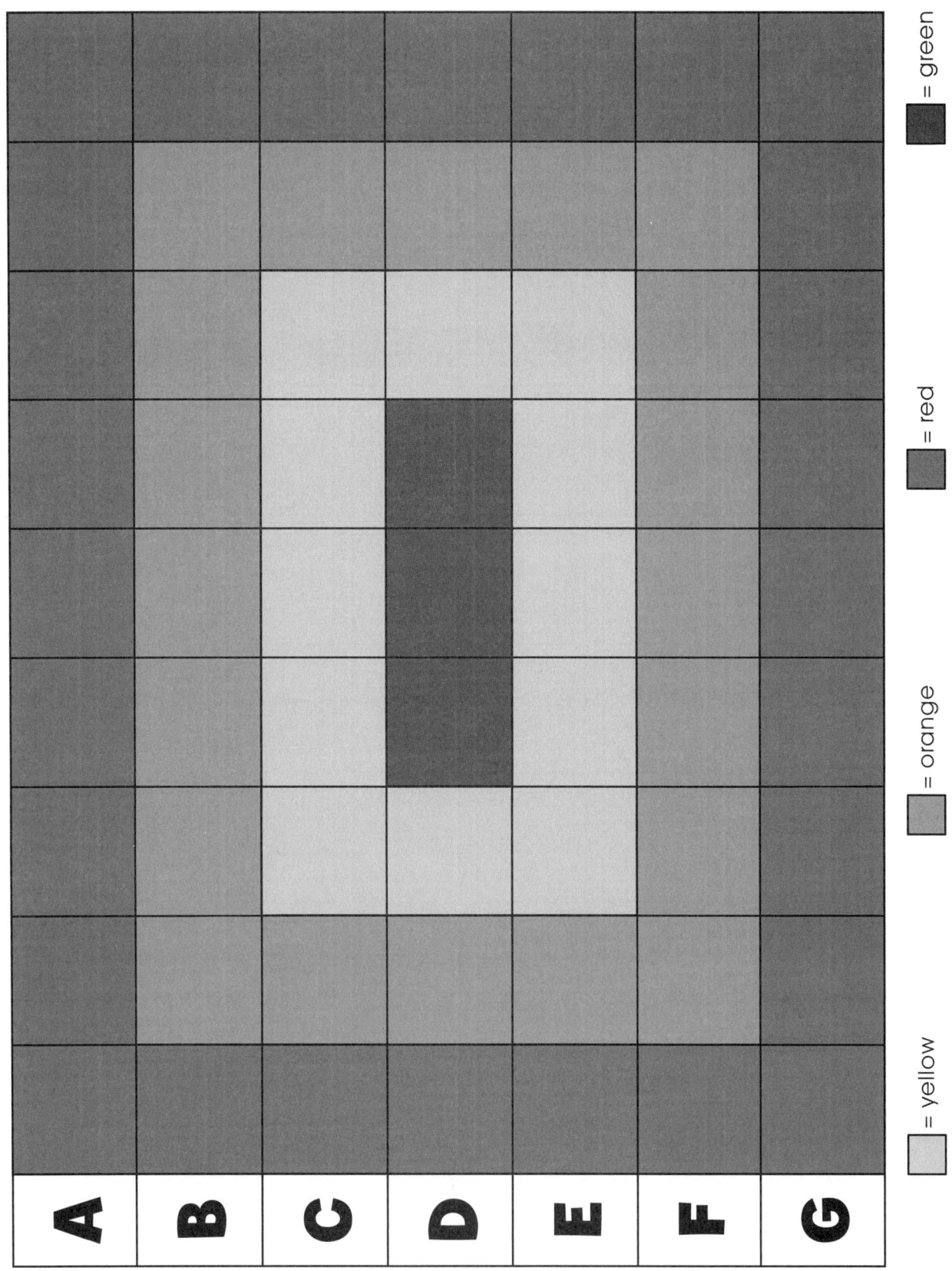

Hidden Picture 2

Directions: Use the information below to color each square on the separate sheet of blank graph paper.

	A	B	C	D	E	F	G
	yellow	yellow	yellow	yellow	yellow/blue	yellow	yellow
	yellow	yellow	yellow	yellow/blue	blue	yellow	yellow
	yellow	yellow	yellow/blue	blue	blue	yellow	yellow
	yellow	yellow/blue	blue	blue/red	blue	yellow	yellow
	yellow/blue	blue	blue/red	red	blue	yellow	yellow
	yellow	yellow/blue	blue	blue/red	blue	yellow	yellow
	yellow	yellow	yellow/blue	blue	blue	yellow	yellow
	yellow	yellow	yellow	yellow/blue	blue	yellow	yellow
	yellow	yellow	yellow	yellow	yellow/blue	yellow	yellow

Hidden Picture 2

Answer Key: Triangles

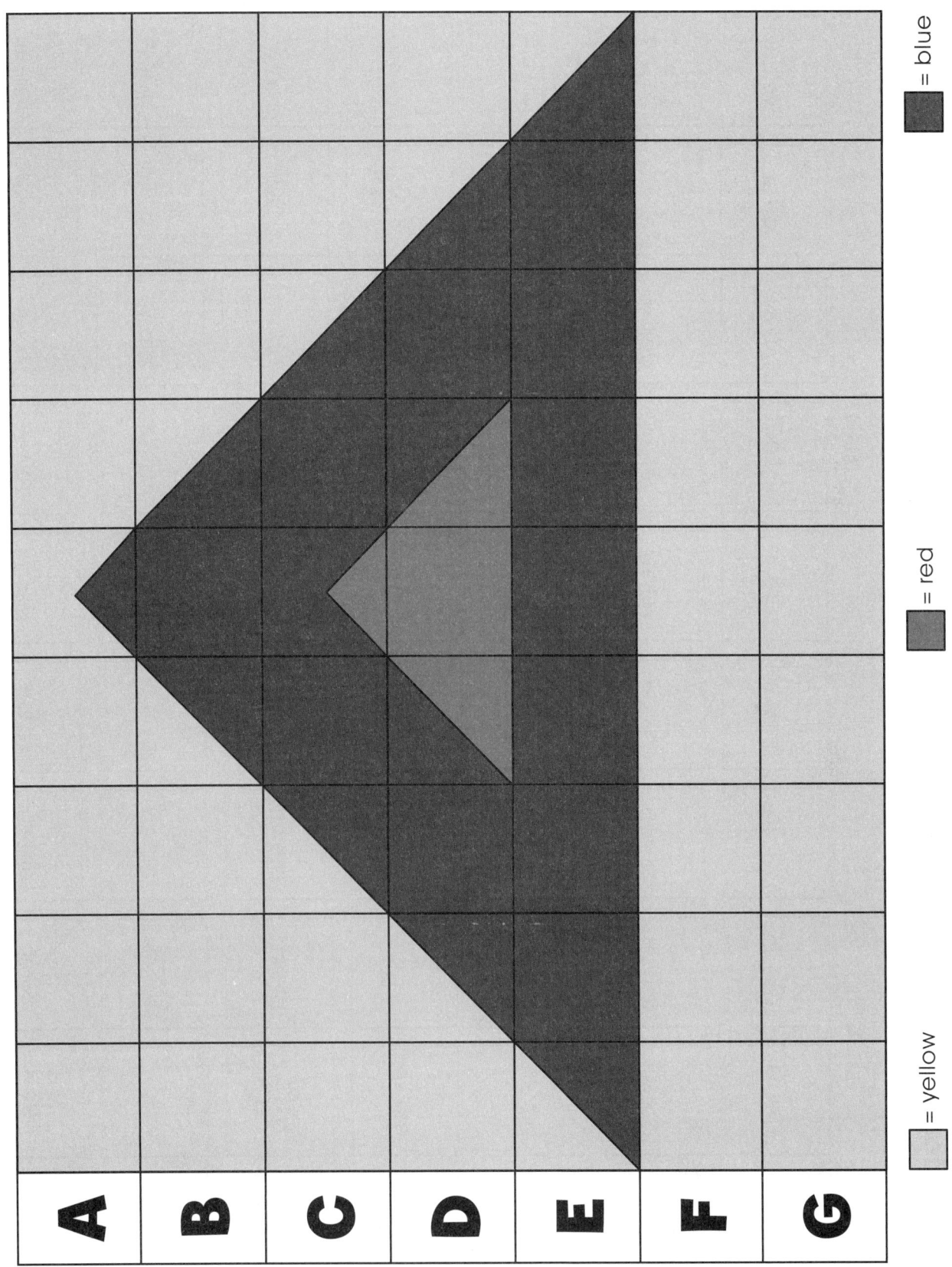

Hidden Picture 3 — Directions

Directions: Use the information below to color each square on the separate sheet of blank graph paper. Draw one eye. Draw a mouth.

	A	B	C	D	E	F	G
1	yellow	yellow/brown	brown	brown	brown	brown/yellow	yellow
2	yellow/brown	brown/yellow	yellow	yellow/brown	brown	brown	brown
3	yellow	yellow	yellow/brown	brown	brown	brown	yellow/brown
4	yellow	yellow	brown	brown	brown	brown	yellow
5	yellow	yellow	brown	brown	brown	brown	yellow
6	yellow	yellow	yellow/brown	brown	brown	brown	yellow
7	yellow/brown	brown	yellow	yellow/brown	brown	brown/yellow	brown
8	yellow/brown	brown	brown/yellow	yellow/brown	brown	brown/yellow	yellow/brown
9	yellow	yellow/brown	brown	brown	brown/yellow	yellow	yellow

© Carson-Dellosa • CD-104282 — Early Graphing Hidden Pictures

Hidden Picture 3

Answer Key: Dinosaur

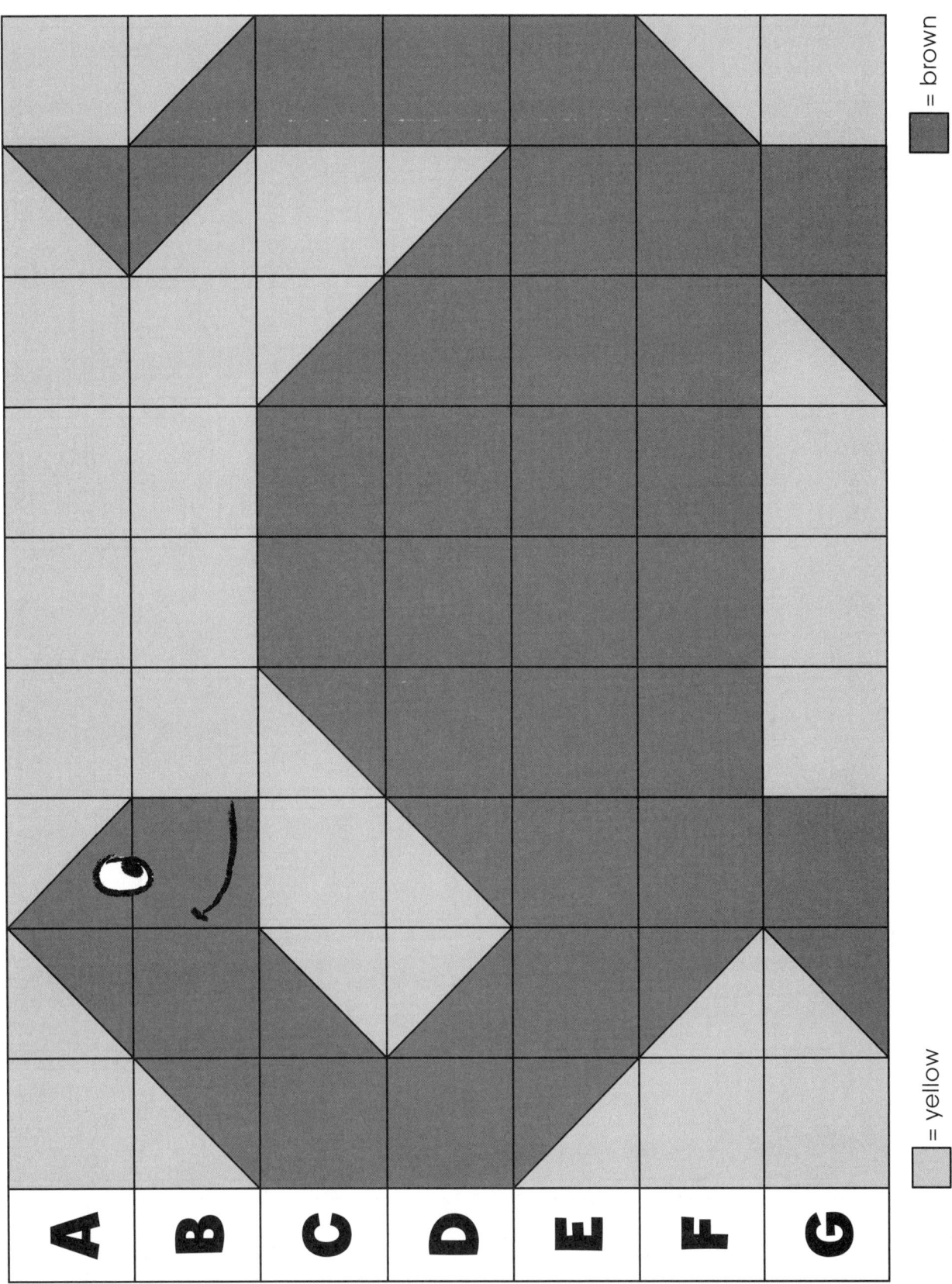

Hidden Picture 4 — Directions

Directions: Use the information below to color each square on the separate sheet of blank graph paper.

A	B	C	D	E	F	G
yellow	red / yellow	yellow / red	red	red / yellow	yellow / red	yellow
yellow	red	red	red	red	red	yellow
yellow	red	red	red	red	red	yellow
yellow	red	red	red	red	red	yellow
yellow	yellow / red	red	red	red	red / yellow	yellow
yellow	green / yellow	yellow	green	yellow	yellow / green	yellow
yellow	yellow / green	green / yellow	green	yellow / green	green / yellow	yellow
yellow	yellow	yellow / green	green	green / yellow	yellow	yellow
green	green	green	green	green	green	green
A	**B**	**C**	**D**	**E**	**F**	**G**

Hidden Picture 4

Answer Key: Tulip

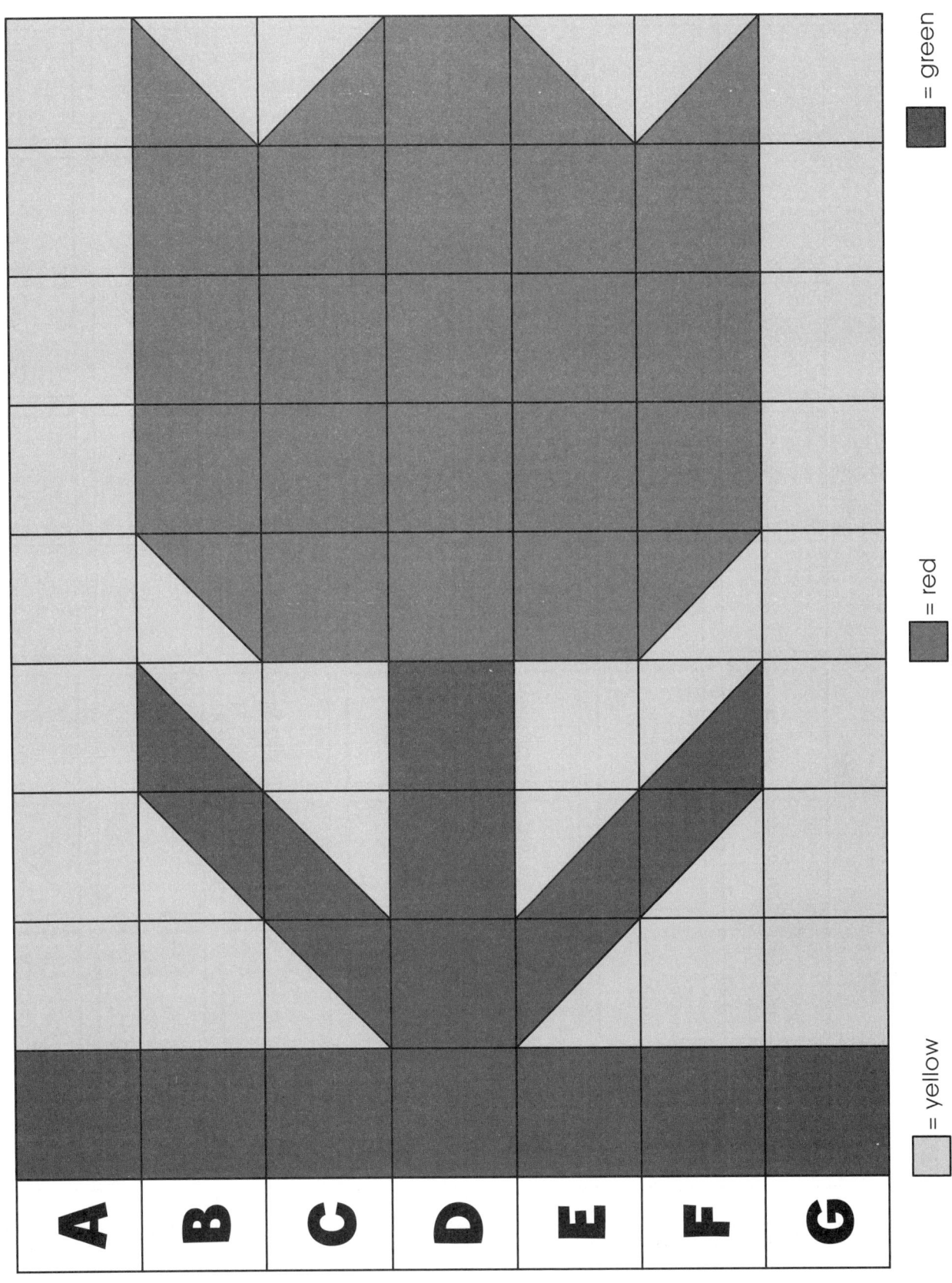

Hidden Picture 5 — Directions

Directions: Use the information below to color each square on the separate sheet of blank graph paper. Draw a nose. Draw a mouth. Draw whiskers.

	A	B	C	D	E	F	G
1	orange/brown	orange	brown/orange	orange	orange	orange/brown	orange
2	orange/brown	brown/orange	brown	brown / yellow	brown / yellow	brown	orange
3	orange/brown	brown/orange	orange/brown	brown	brown	brown/orange	orange
4	brown	orange	orange	orange | brown	brown | orange	orange	orange
5	brown	orange/brown	brown	brown	brown	brown	brown/orange
6	orange/brown	brown	brown	brown	brown	brown	brown
7	orange	orange/brown	brown	brown	brown	brown	brown/orange
8	orange	orange	brown	orange/brown	brown/orange	brown	orange
9	orange	orange/brown	brown	brown/orange	orange/brown	brown	brown/orange

Hidden Picture 5

Answer Key: Cat

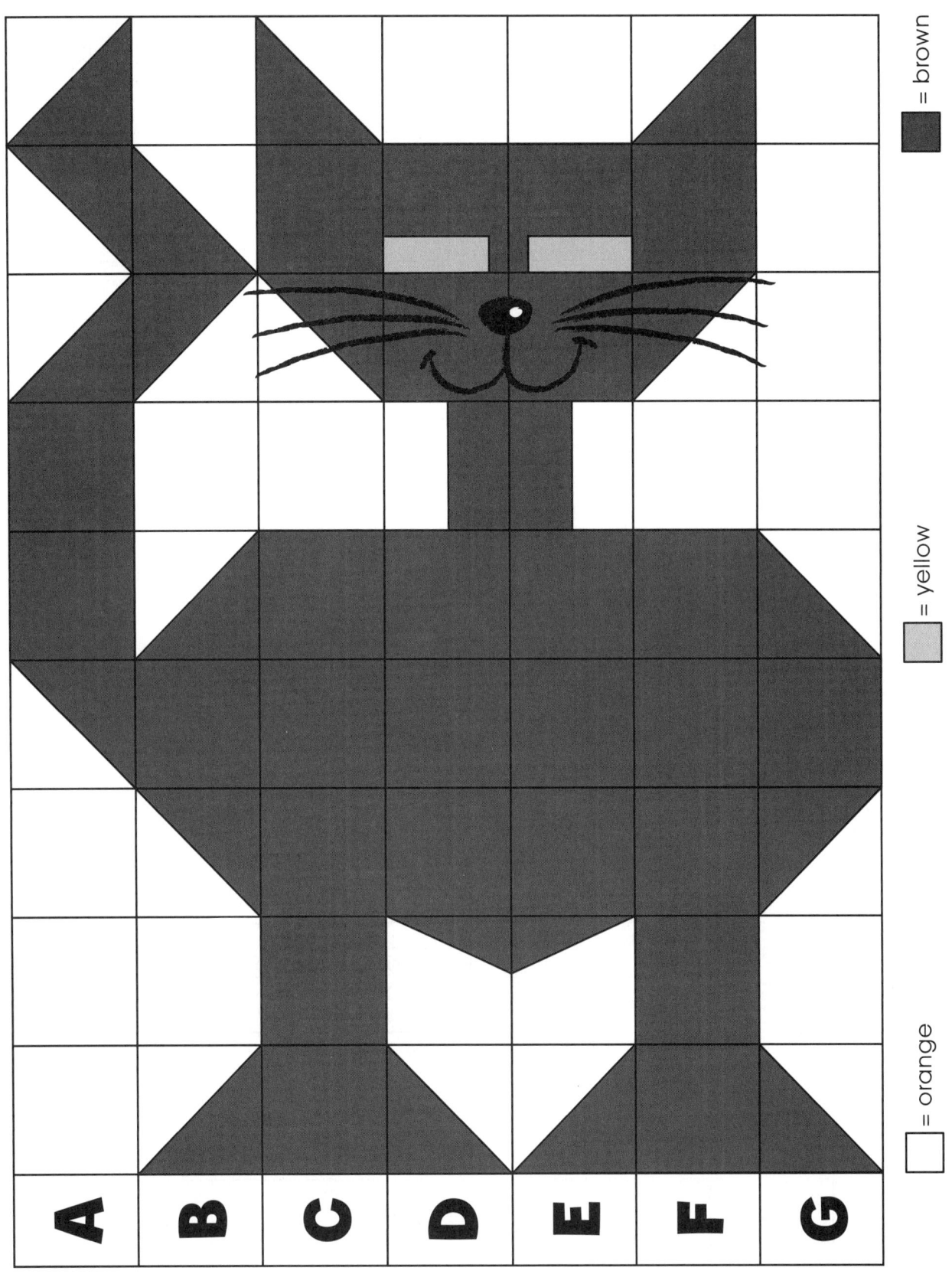

Hidden Picture 6

Directions: Use the information below to color each square on the separate sheet of blank graph paper. Draw one eye. Draw whiskers. Draw a long, black tail.

	A	B	C	D	E	F	G
7	yellow	yellow	yellow	yellow	yellow	green	green
6	yellow	yellow	yellow	yellow	yellow	green	green
5	yellow	yellow	yellow/gray	gray	gray/yellow	green	green
4	yellow	yellow	gray	gray	gray	green	green
3	yellow	yellow	gray	gray	gray	green	green
2	yellow	yellow	yellow/gray	gray	gray	green	green
1	yellow	yellow/pink	pink	pink/gray	gray	green	green
0	yellow	yellow/pink	pink	pink/yellow	yellow/gray	green	green
	yellow	yellow	yellow	yellow	yellow	green	green

Hidden Picture 6

Answer Key: Mouse

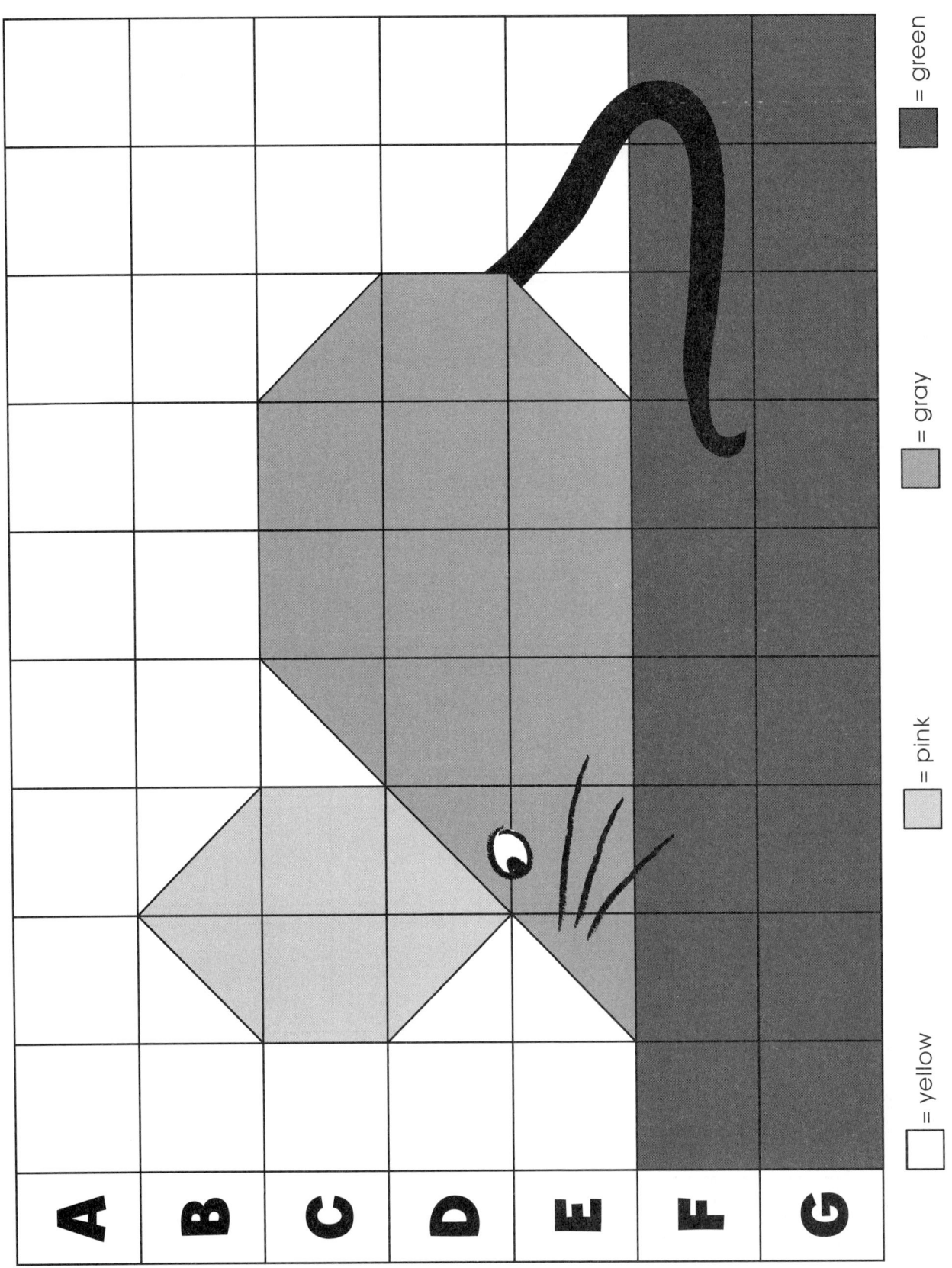

Hidden Picture 7 — Directions

Directions: Use the information below to color each square on the separate sheet of blank graph paper.

	A	B	C	D	E	F	G
9	pink	pink	pink/black	pink	pink	green	green
8	pink	pink/gray	gray	gray	gray/pink	green	green
7	pink	gray	gray	gray	gray	black	black
6	pink	gray	gray	gray	gray	green	green
5	pink	gray	gray	gray	gray	green	green
4	pink	pink/gray	gray	gray	gray	black	black
3	pink/gray	gray/black	gray	gray	gray/pink	green	green
2	gray	gray/green	gray	pink	pink	green	green
1	pink/gray	gray	black	pink	pink	green	green

Hidden Picture 7

Answer Key: Lamb

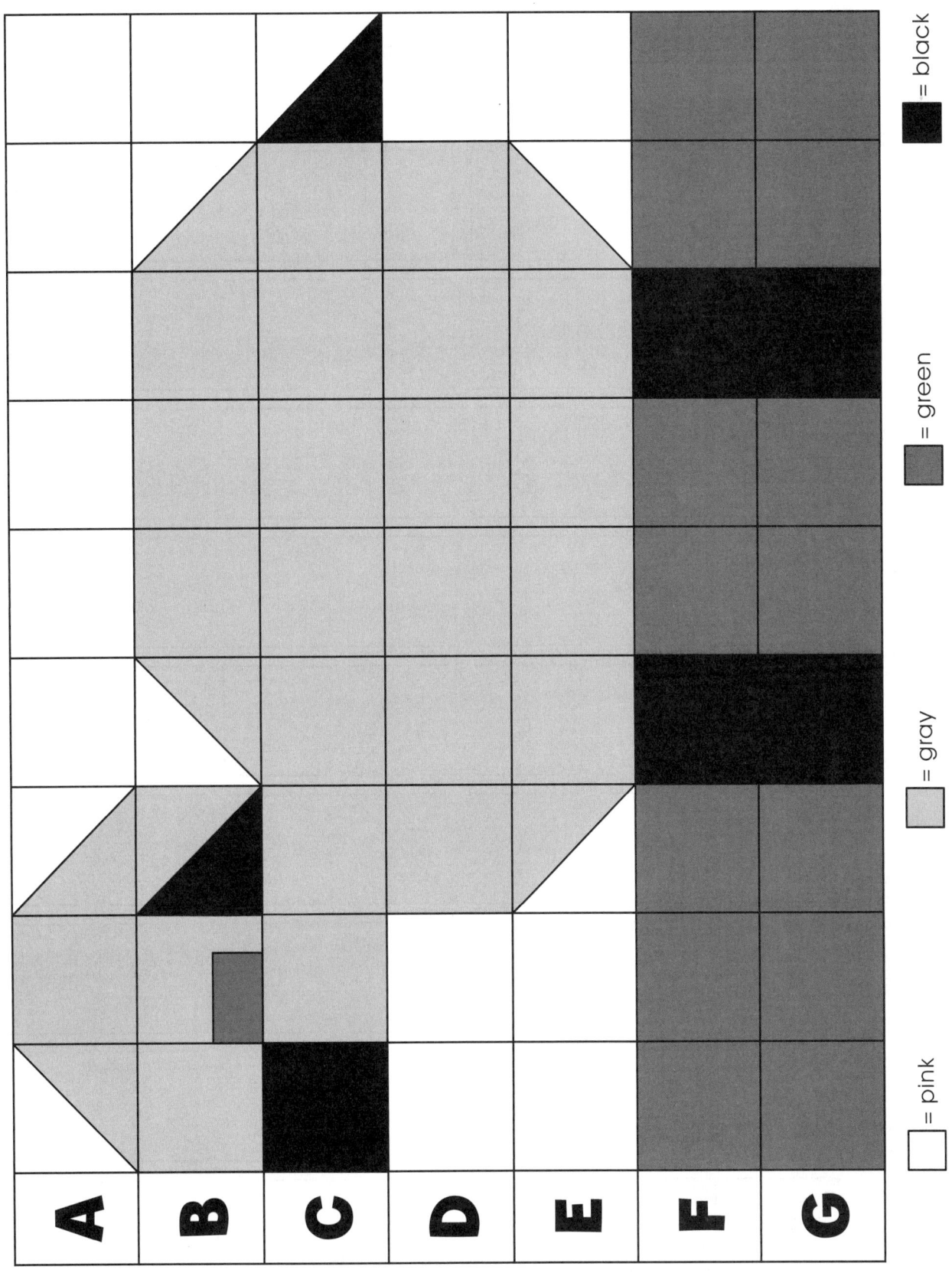

Hidden Picture 8

Directions

Directions: Use the information below to color each square on the separate sheet of blank graph paper. Draw antennae.

	A	B	C	D	E	F	G
9	green	green	green	green	green	green	green
8	green	green	green	green	green/black	black/green	green
7	green	green	green	green/yellow	yellow	yellow	yellow/green
6	green	gray	gray/green	black	black	black	black
5	green	green/gray	gray	yellow	yellow	yellow	yellow
4	green/gray	gray	gray	gray/black	black	black	black/green
3	green/gray	gray	gray	gray/black	black	black/green	green
2	green	green	green	black	black	black	green
1	green	green	green	green/black	yellow/black	black/green	green

Hidden Picture 8

Answer Key: Bumblebee

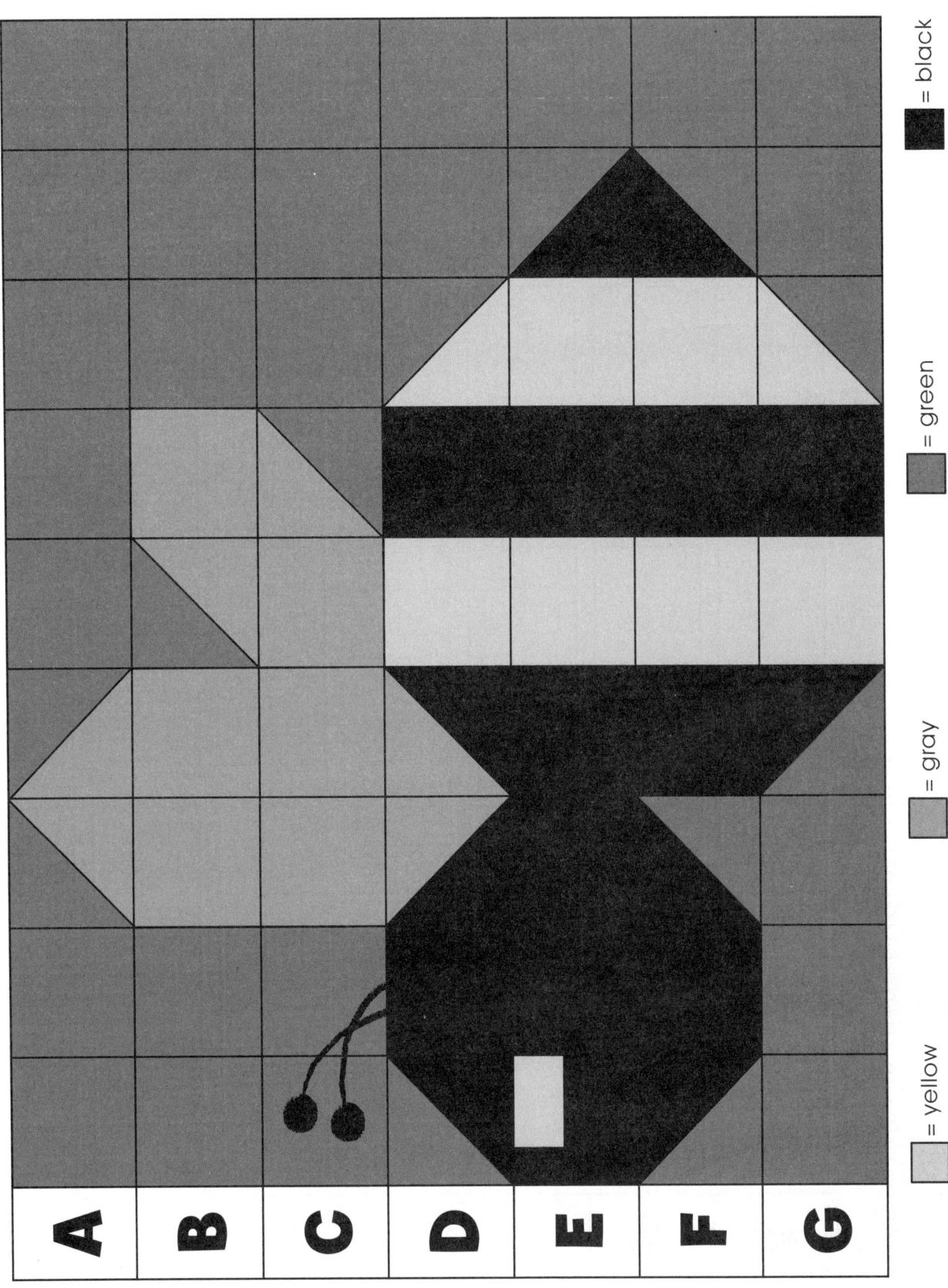

Hidden Picture 9

Directions: Use the information below to color each square on the separate sheet of blank graph paper. Draw a mouth. Draw legs.

	A	B	C	D	E	F	G
1	orange	orange/green	green/orange	orange/green	green	green/orange	brown
2	orange	green	green	green	green	green	brown
3	orange	orange/green	green/orange	orange/green	green	green/orange	brown
4	orange	orange	orange	orange/green	green	green/orange	brown
5	orange	orange	orange	green	green	green	brown
6	orange	orange	orange	orange/green	green	green/orange	brown
7	orange/green	green/black	green/orange	orange/green	green	green/orange	brown
8	green	green	green	green	green	green	brown
9	orange/green	green/black	green/orange	orange/green	green	green/orange	brown

Hidden Picture 9

Answer Key: Caterpillar

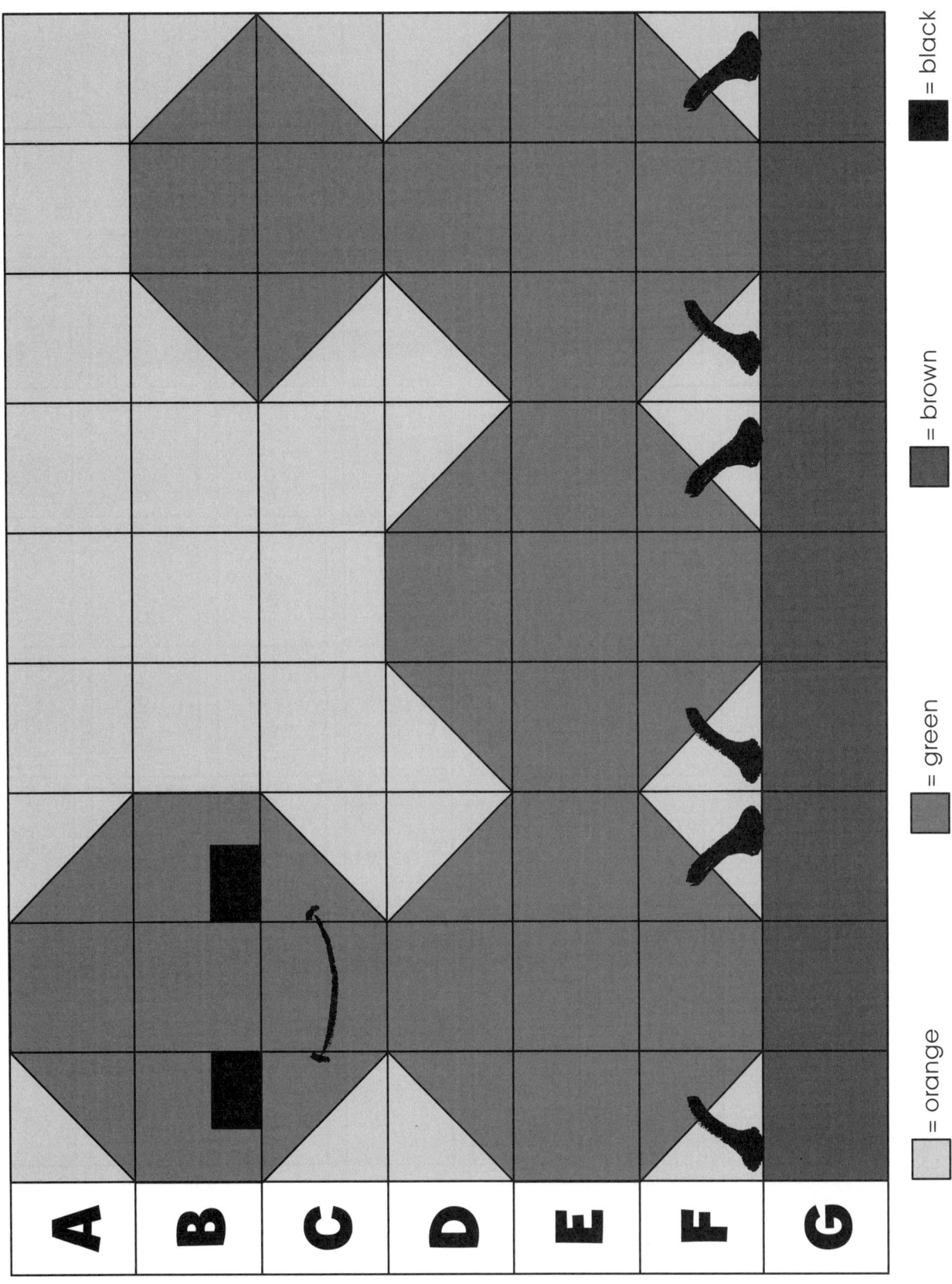

Hidden Picture 10 — Directions

Directions: Use the information below to color each square on the separate sheet of blank graph paper. Draw a face. Draw antennae.

	A	B	C	D	E	F	G
9	blue	blue	blue	blue	blue	blue	blue
8	blue	blue/orange	orange	orange/blue	blue/orange	orange/blue	blue
7	blue	orange	purple	orange	orange	purple	orange/blue
6	blue	blue/orange	orange	orange	orange	orange	orange/blue
5	blue	green	green	green	green	green	green
4	blue	blue/orange	orange	orange	orange	orange	orange/blue
3	blue	orange	purple	orange	orange	purple	orange/blue
2	blue	blue/orange	orange	orange/blue	blue/orange	orange/blue	blue
1	blue	blue	blue	blue	blue	blue	blue

Hidden Picture 10

Answer Key: Butterfly

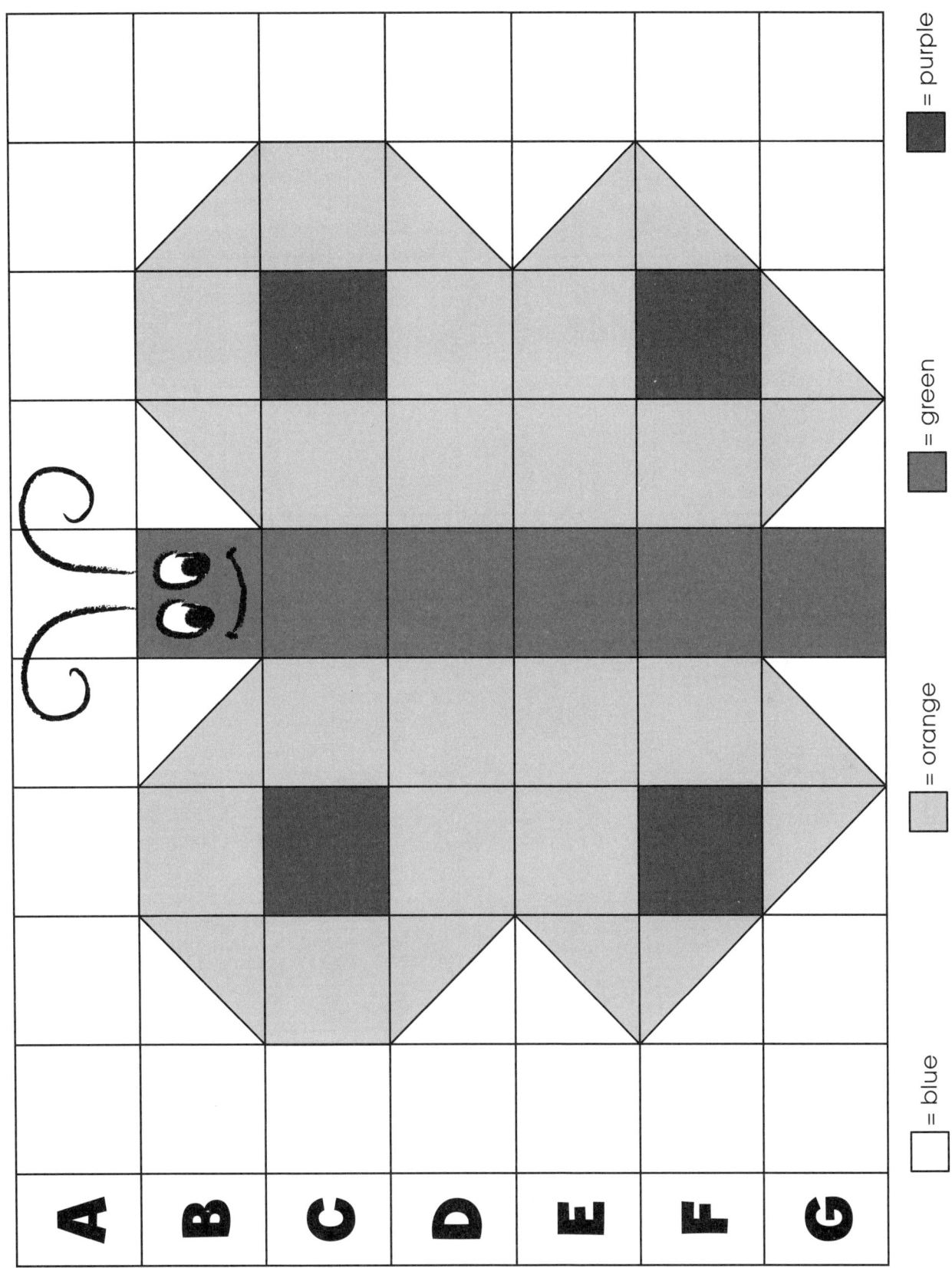

Hidden Picture 11 — Directions

Directions: Use the information below to color each square on the separate sheet of blank graph paper. Draw a face.

	A	B	C	D	E	F	G
9	green	green	green	purple/green	green/purple	green	green
8	green	green	green/black	black	black	black/green	green
7	green	green	black	brown	brown	black	green
6	green	green	black	brown	brown	black	green
5	green	brown	purple	orange/purple	purple/orange	purple	brown
4	green	green	green/purple	purple	purple	purple/green	green
3	green	green/purple	purple	purple	purple	purple	purple/green
2	green	black	black/purple	purple	purple	purple/black	black
1	green	green/black	black	green	green	black	black/green

Hidden Picture 11

Answer Key: Doll

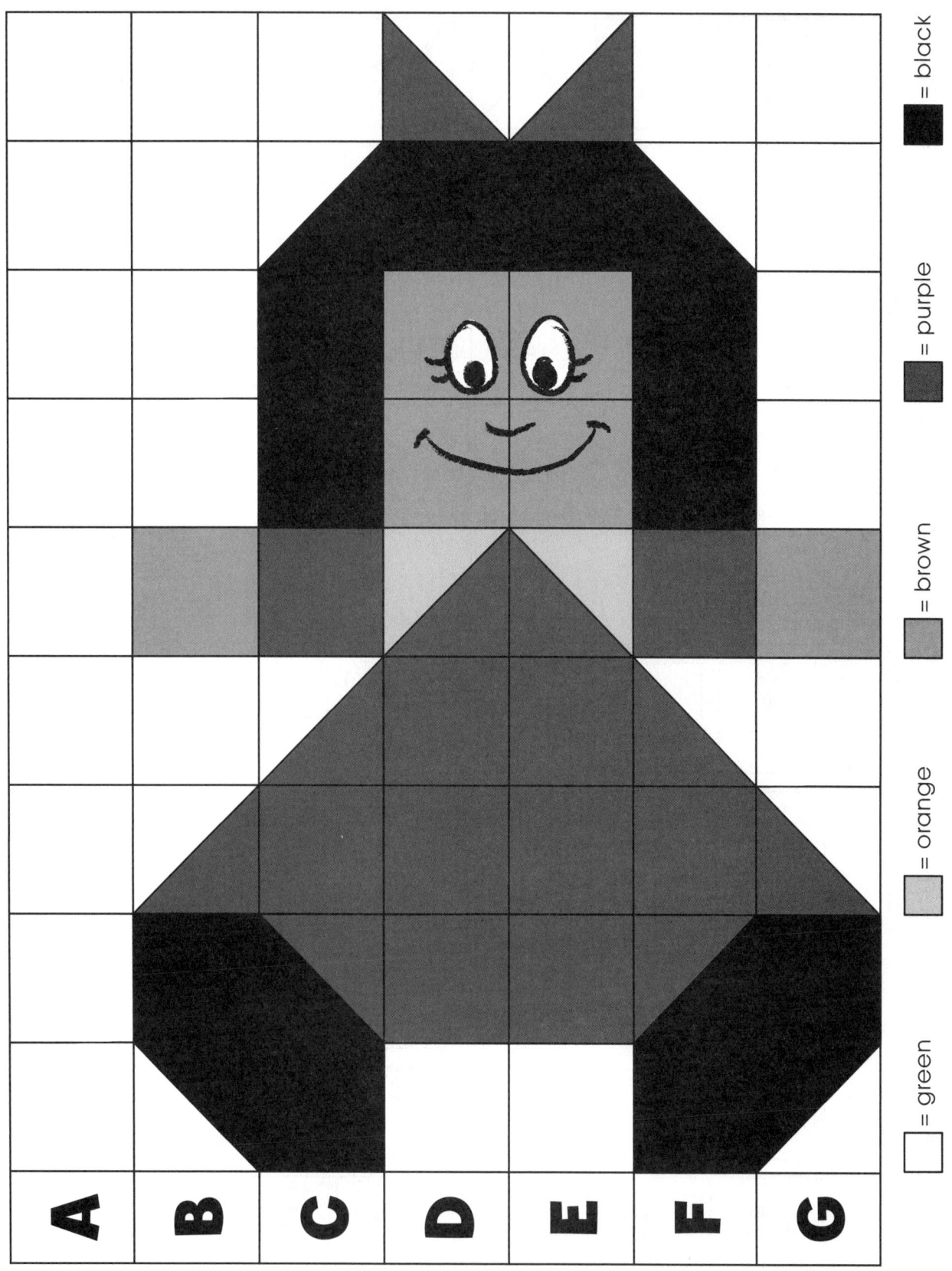

Hidden Picture 12

Directions: Use the information below to color each square on the separate sheet of blank graph paper. Draw eyes, a nose, and a mouth.

	A	B	C	D	E	F	G
9	blue	blue	blue/brown	brown/blue	blue	blue	green
8	blue	blue	blue	brown	brown	brown	green
7	blue	blue	blue	brown	brown	blue/brown	green
6	blue	brown/blue	blue	brown	brown	blue	green
5	blue	brown	brown	brown	brown	brown	green
4	blue	brown	brown	blue	blue/red	blue/brown	green
3	blue	brown/blue	blue/red	red	red	red	green
2	blue	blue	blue/red	red	red	red	green
1	blue	blue	blue	blue	blue/red	blue	green

Hidden Picture 12

Answer Key: Dog and Fire Hydrant

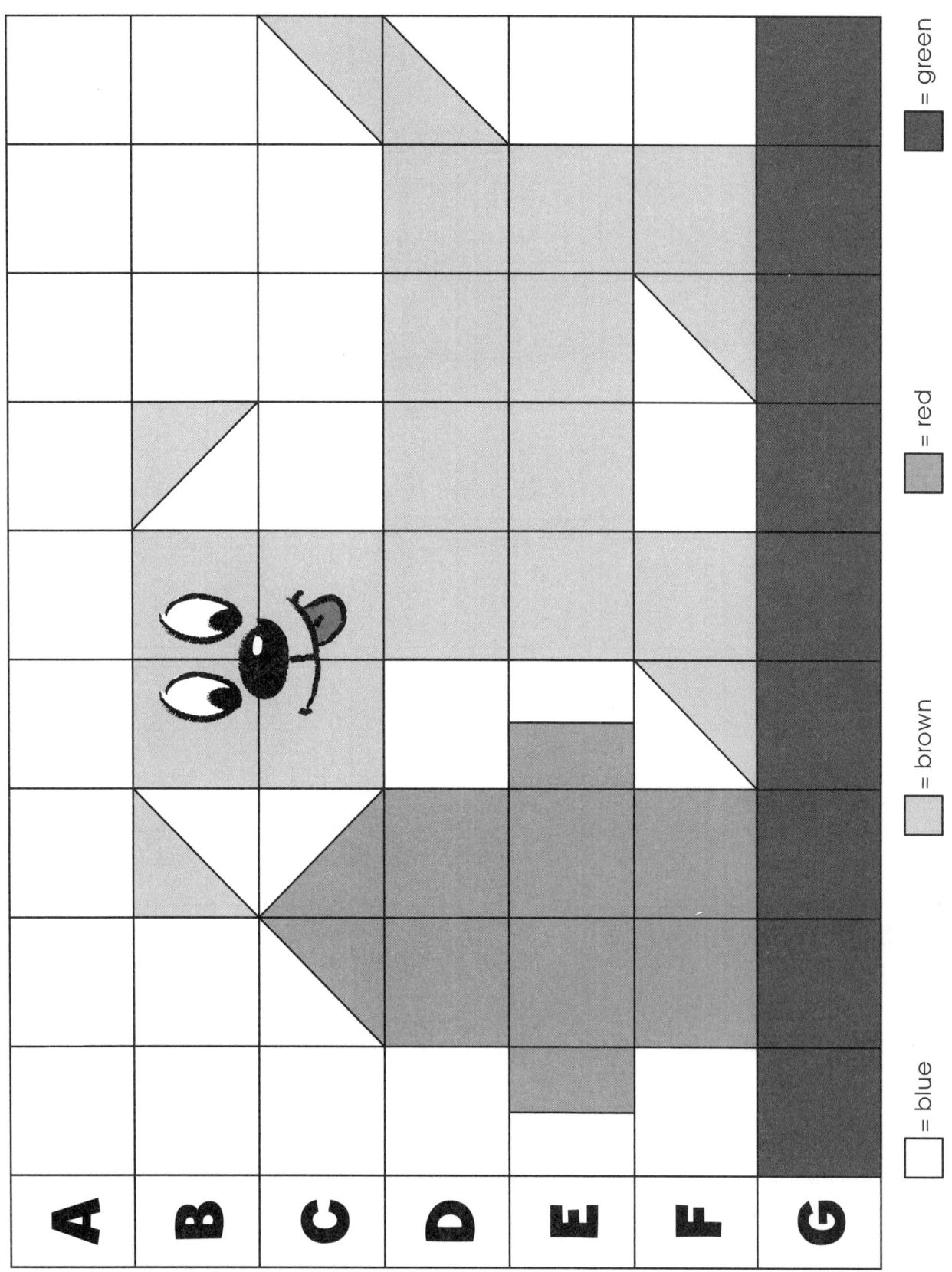

Hidden Picture 13 — Directions

Directions: Use the information below to color each square on the separate sheet of blank graph paper.

	A	B	C	D	E	F	G
1	blue	blue	blue	blue	blue	blue	blue
2	blue	blue/green	green	green	green	green/blue	blue
3	blue	green	green + red	green	green + red	green	blue
4	blue	green + red	green	green + red	green	green	blue
5	blue	blue/green	green + red	green	green + red	green/blue	blue
6	blue	blue	blue	brown	blue	blue	blue
7	blue	blue	blue	brown	blue	blue	blue
8	blue	blue	blue/brown	brown	brown/blue	blue	blue
9	green	green	green	green	green	green	green

Hidden Picture 13

Answer Key: Apple Tree

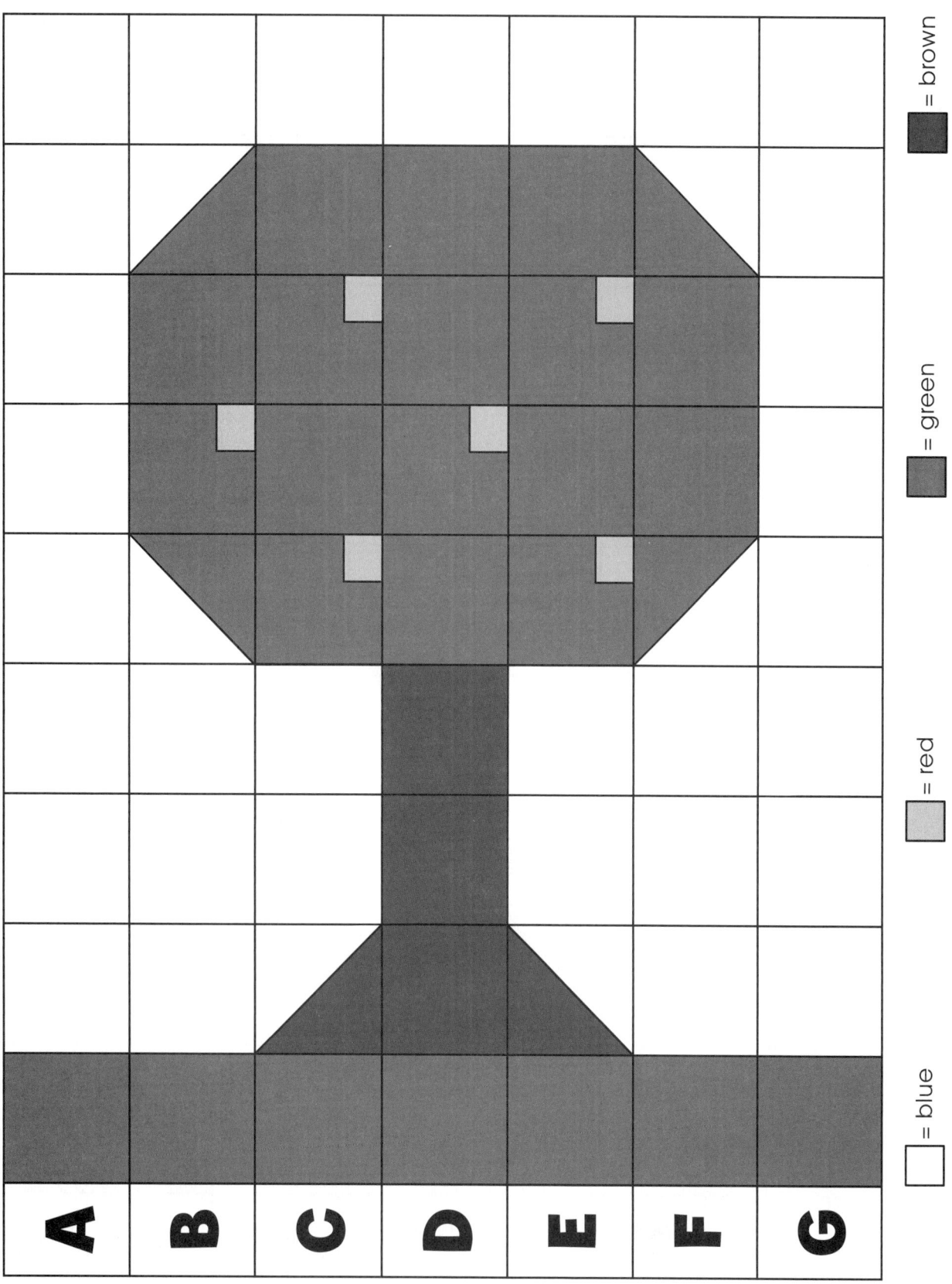

Hidden Picture 14

Directions

Directions: Use the information below to color each square on the separate sheet of blank graph paper.

	A	B	C	D	E	F	G
9	light blue	light blue	light blue	light blue	light blue	light blue	dark blue
8	light blue	light blue	light blue	light blue	red	red	dark blue
7	light blue	light blue	light blue	light blue	red	red	dark blue
6	light blue	light blue	yellow	yellow	red	red	dark blue
5	light blue	red	yellow / black	yellow	red	red	dark blue
4	light blue	light blue	yellow / black	yellow	red	red	dark blue
3	light blue	light blue	light blue	light blue	red	red	dark blue
2	light blue	light blue	light blue	light blue	red	red / light blue	dark blue
1	light blue	light blue	light blue	light blue	red / light blue	light blue	dark blue

Hidden Picture 14

Answer Key: Tugboat

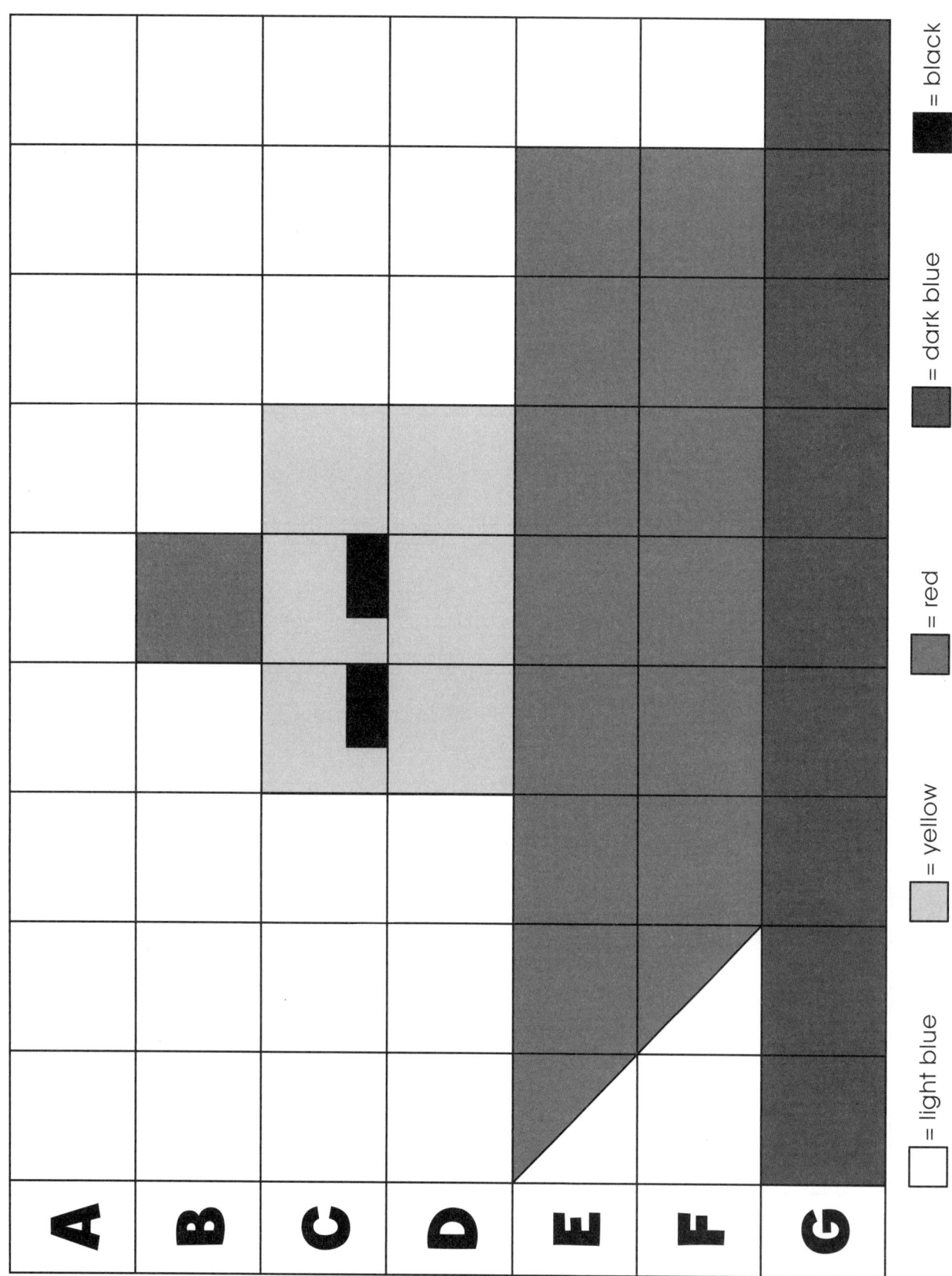

Hidden Picture 15

Directions: Use the information below to color each square on the separate sheet of blank graph paper.

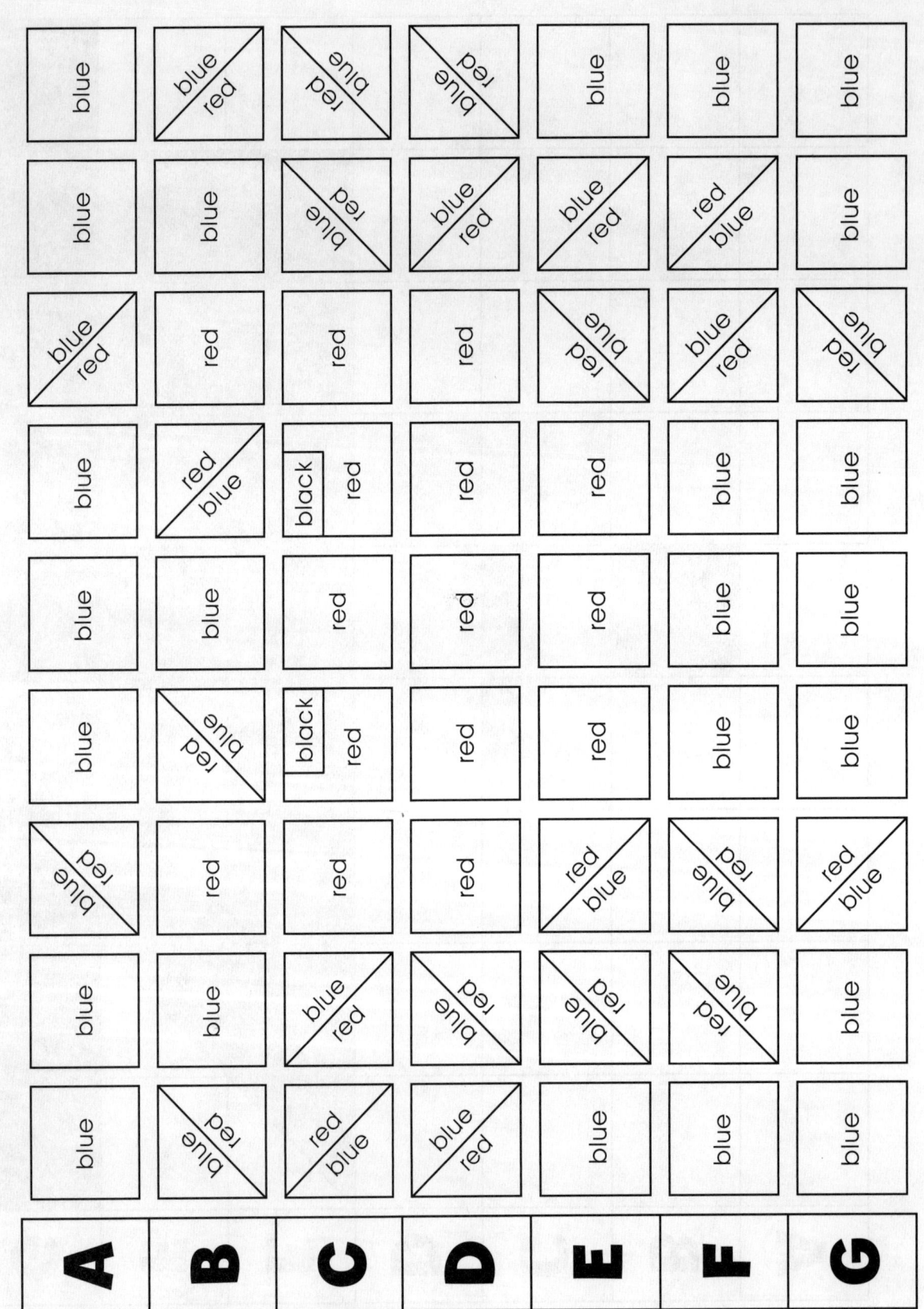

Hidden Picture 15

Answer Key: Crab

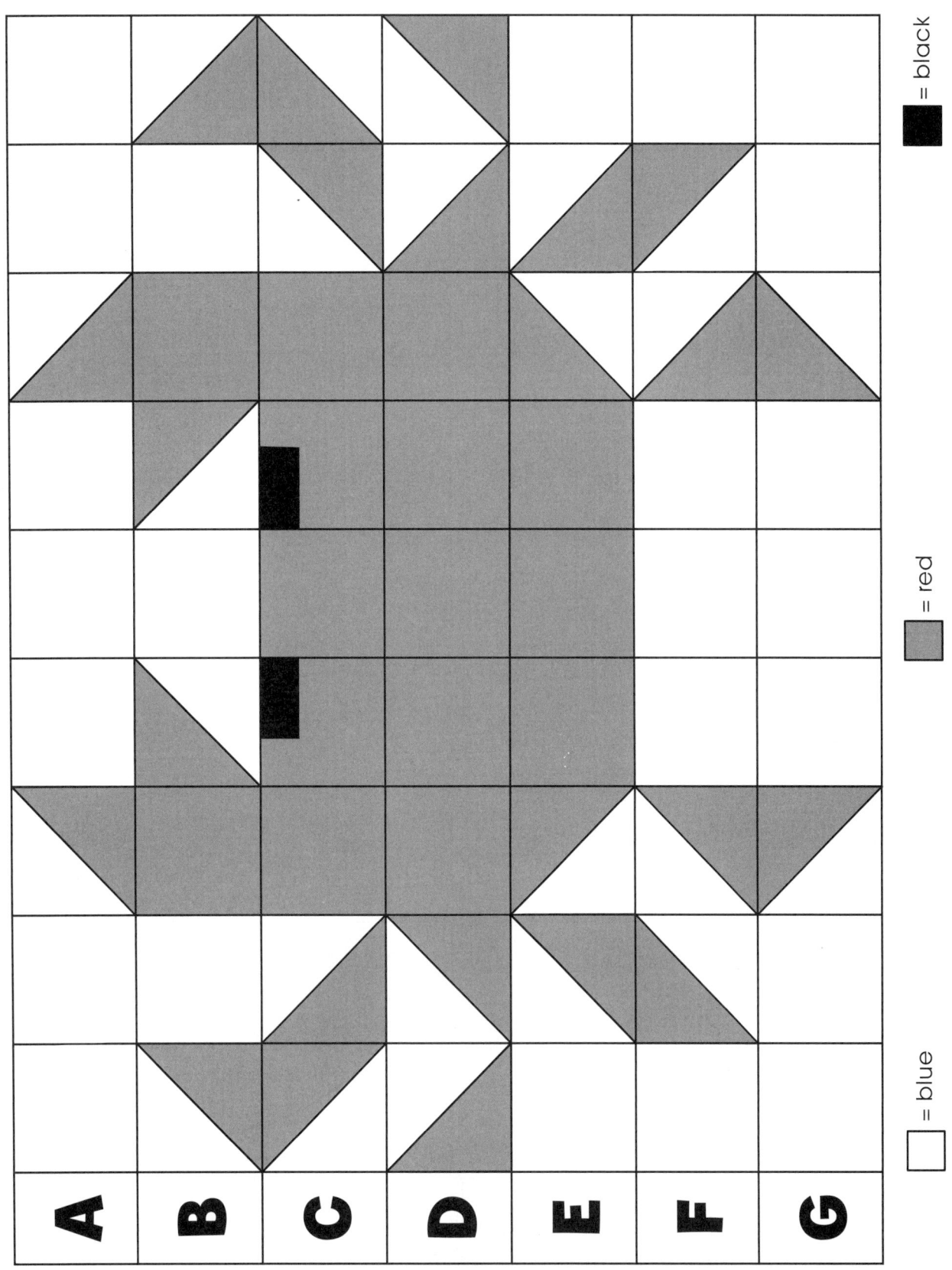

Hidden Picture 16 — Directions

Directions: Use the information below to color each square on the separate sheet of blank graph paper. Draw a mouth. Draw water coming from a blowhole.

	A	B	C	D	E	F	G
1	gray	gray / light blue	light blue	light blue	light blue	light blue	dark blue
2	light blue / gray	gray	gray	gray	gray	gray / light blue	dark blue
3	light blue / gray	gray	gray	gray	gray	gray	dark blue
4	gray	gray / light blue	light blue	light blue	gray	gray	dark blue
5	light blue	light blue / gray	gray	gray	gray	gray	dark blue
6	light blue	gray	gray	gray	gray	gray	dark blue
7	light blue	gray	gray	gray	gray	gray	dark blue
8	light blue	gray	gray / black	gray	gray	gray	dark blue
9	light blue	light blue / gray	gray	gray	gray	gray / light blue	dark blue

© Carson-Dellosa • CD-104282   Early Graphing Hidden Pictures

Hidden Picture 16

Answer Key: Whale

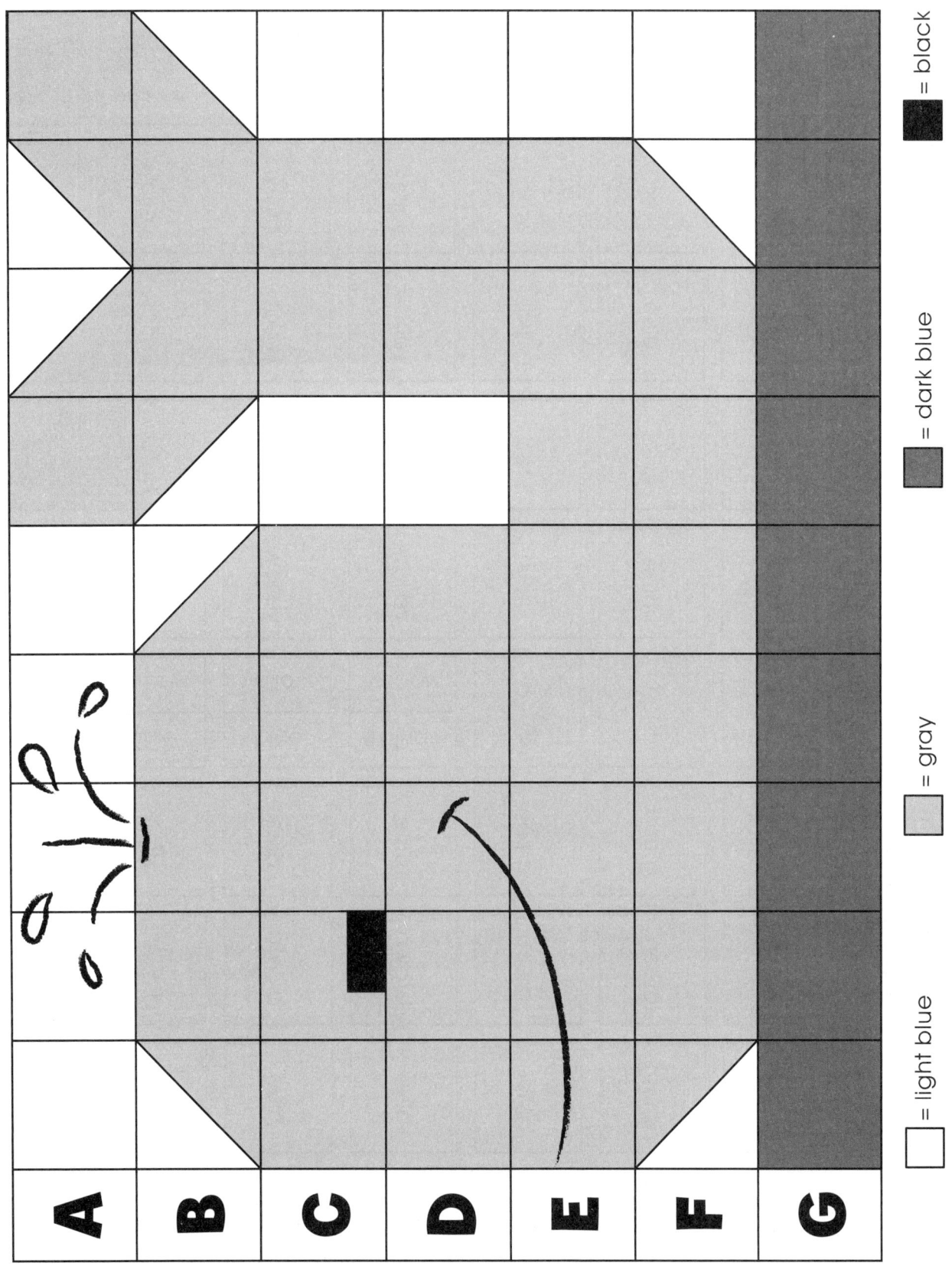

Hidden Picture 17

Directions: Use the information below to color each square on the separate sheet of blank graph paper.

Row	A	B	C	D	E	F	G
9	blue	blue	blue/red	blue/yellow	blue/yellow	blue/yellow	green
8	blue	red	red	yellow	brown	yellow	green
7	blue	blue	red	yellow	yellow	yellow	green
6	blue	blue	red	yellow	brown	brown	green
5	blue	blue	red	yellow	yellow	yellow	green
4	blue	blue	blue/red	blue/yellow	blue/yellow	blue/yellow	green
3	blue/green	green	green	blue	blue	blue	green
2	green	green	green	brown	brown	brown	green
1	blue/green	green	green	blue	blue	blue	green

© Carson-Dellosa • CD-104282
Early Graphing Hidden Pictures

Hidden Picture 17

Answer Key: House and Tree

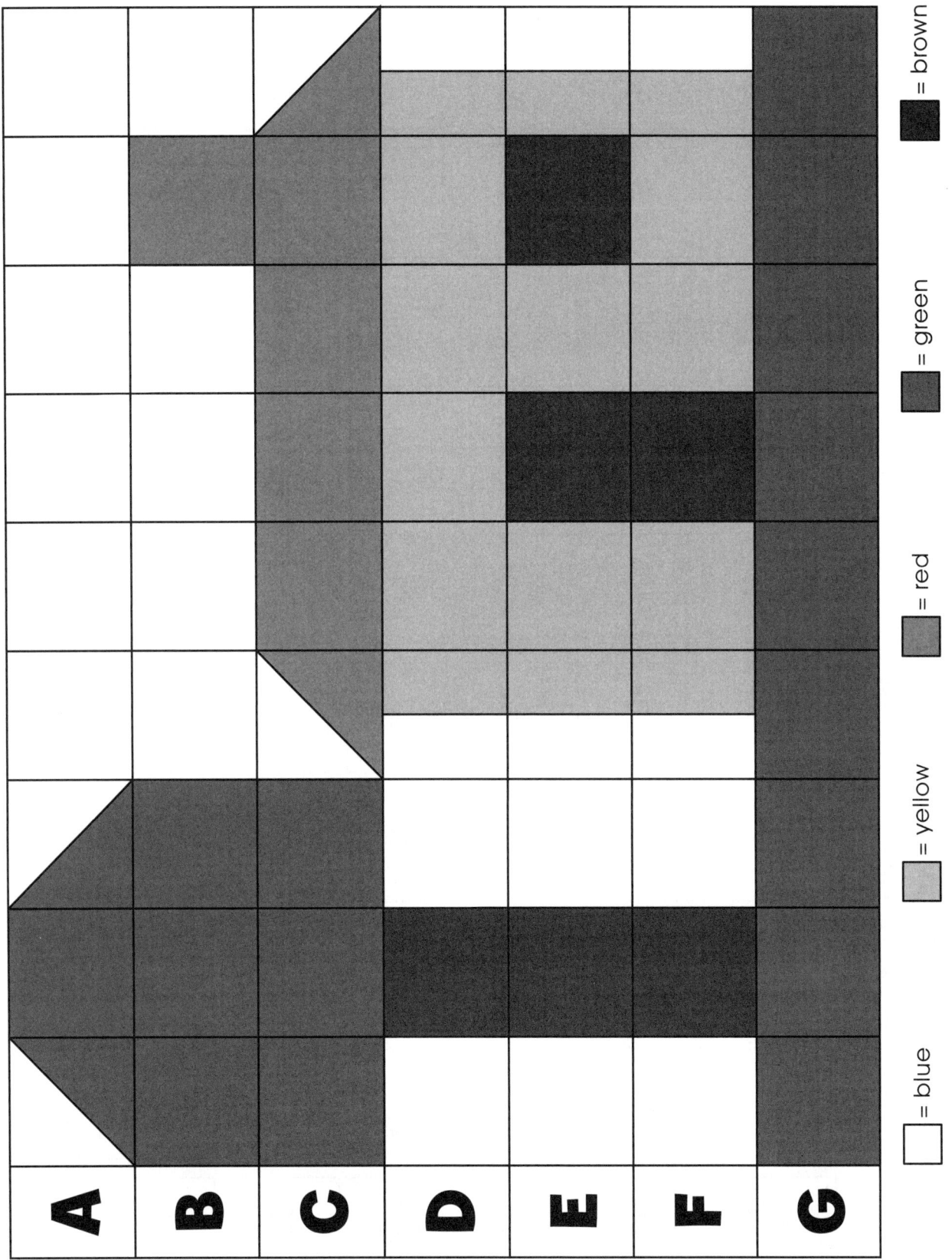

Hidden Picture 18 — Directions

Directions: Use the information below to color each square on the separate sheet of blank graph paper. Draw one eye and an eyebrow. Draw a mouth.

	A	B	C	D	E	F	G
1	blue	blue/white	white	white	white/brown	brown/white	white
2	blue	blue	white	white	white	white/brown	brown/white
3	blue	blue	blue/white	white	white/black	black	brown
4	blue	blue	blue	white	white	green	brown
5	blue/red	pink	pink/blue	white	white	green	brown
6	red	red	yellow	red	red	red	green
7	blue/red	red	yellow	green/red	red	red/green	brown
8	blue	blue	blue/white	green	white/red	red	brown
9	blue	blue	white	white/green	white	white	brown/white

Hidden Picture 18 Answer Key: Sledder

Hidden Picture 19

Directions: Use the information below to color each square on the separate sheet of blank graph paper.

	A	B	C	D	E	F	G
1	blue	blue	blue	blue / yellow	yellow / blue	blue	blue
2	blue	blue	blue / red	red / yellow	yellow	yellow / blue	blue
3	blue	blue / yellow	yellow / red	red	red / yellow	yellow	blue
4	blue	red / yellow	yellow	yellow / red	red / blue	yellow	blue
5	blue	blue / red / red	red / yellow	yellow / yellow / blue	blue	blue	blue
6	blue	red / yellow	yellow	yellow / red	blue / red	yellow	blue
7	blue	blue / yellow	yellow / red	red	red / yellow	yellow	blue
8	blue	blue	blue / red	red / yellow	yellow	yellow / blue	blue
9	blue	blue	blue	blue / yellow	yellow / blue	blue	blue

Hidden Picture 19

Answer Key: Mittens

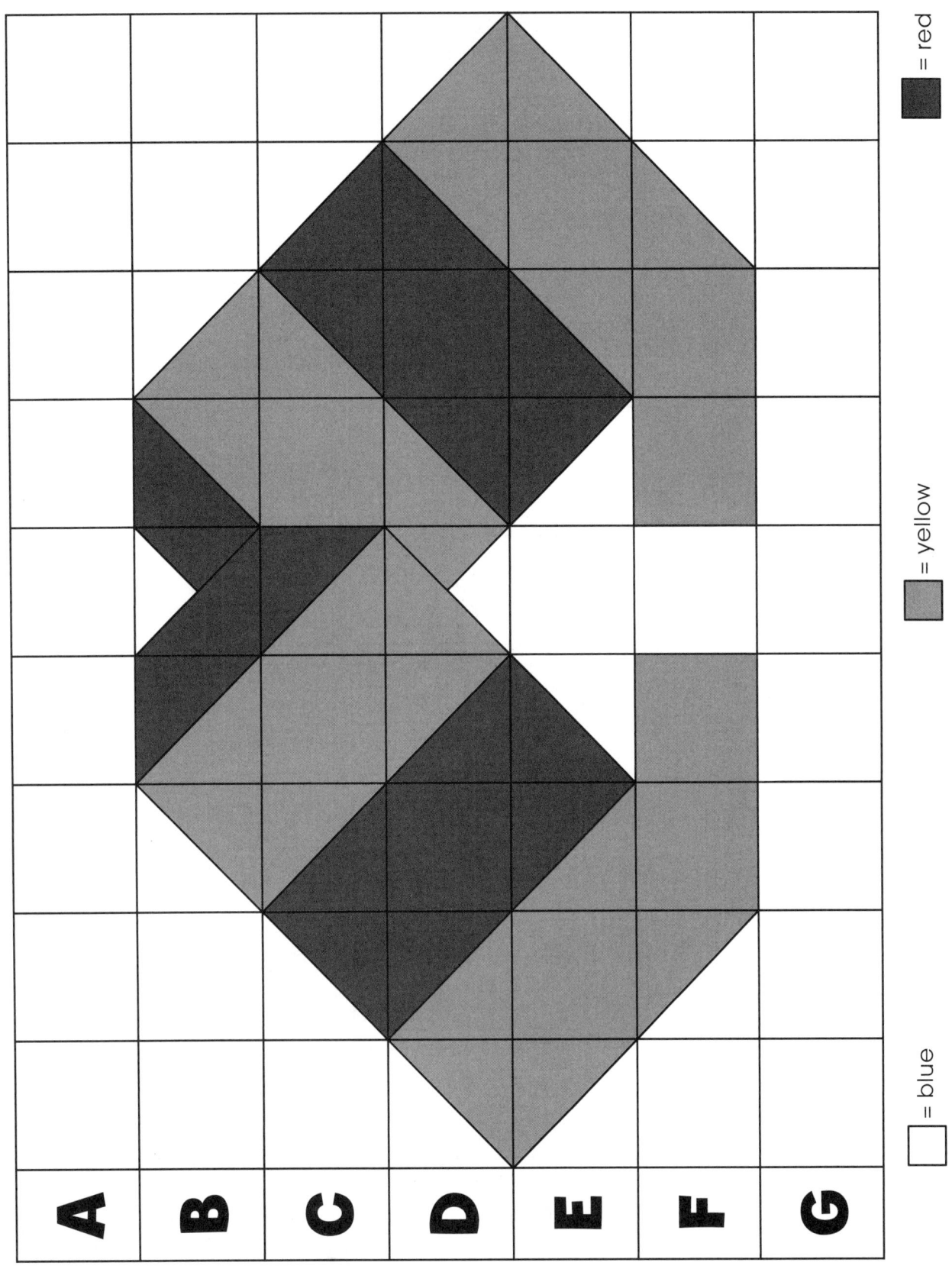

Hidden Picture 20 — Directions

Directions: Use the information below to color each square on the separate sheet of blank graph paper. Draw an ear. Draw a mouth. Draw teeth.

	A	B	C	D	E	F	G
1	blue	blue	blue / light brown	light brown (black)	light brown	light brown / blue	blue
2	blue	blue	blue / light brown	light brown	light brown	light brown	blue
3	blue	blue	blue	blue / light brown	light brown	light brown	light brown / blue
4	blue	blue	light brown	light brown	light brown	light brown	light brown
5	blue	blue	blue	yellow	yellow	light brown	light brown
6	blue	blue	blue / dark brown	yellow / light brown	light brown	light brown	light brown
7	blue	blue	dark brown	light brown	light brown	light brown	light brown
8	green / blue	green / blue	green / dark brown	dark brown / light brown	light brown	light brown	light brown / green
9	green	green	dark brown	light brown	light brown	light brown	green

Hidden Picture 20

Answer Key: Groundhog

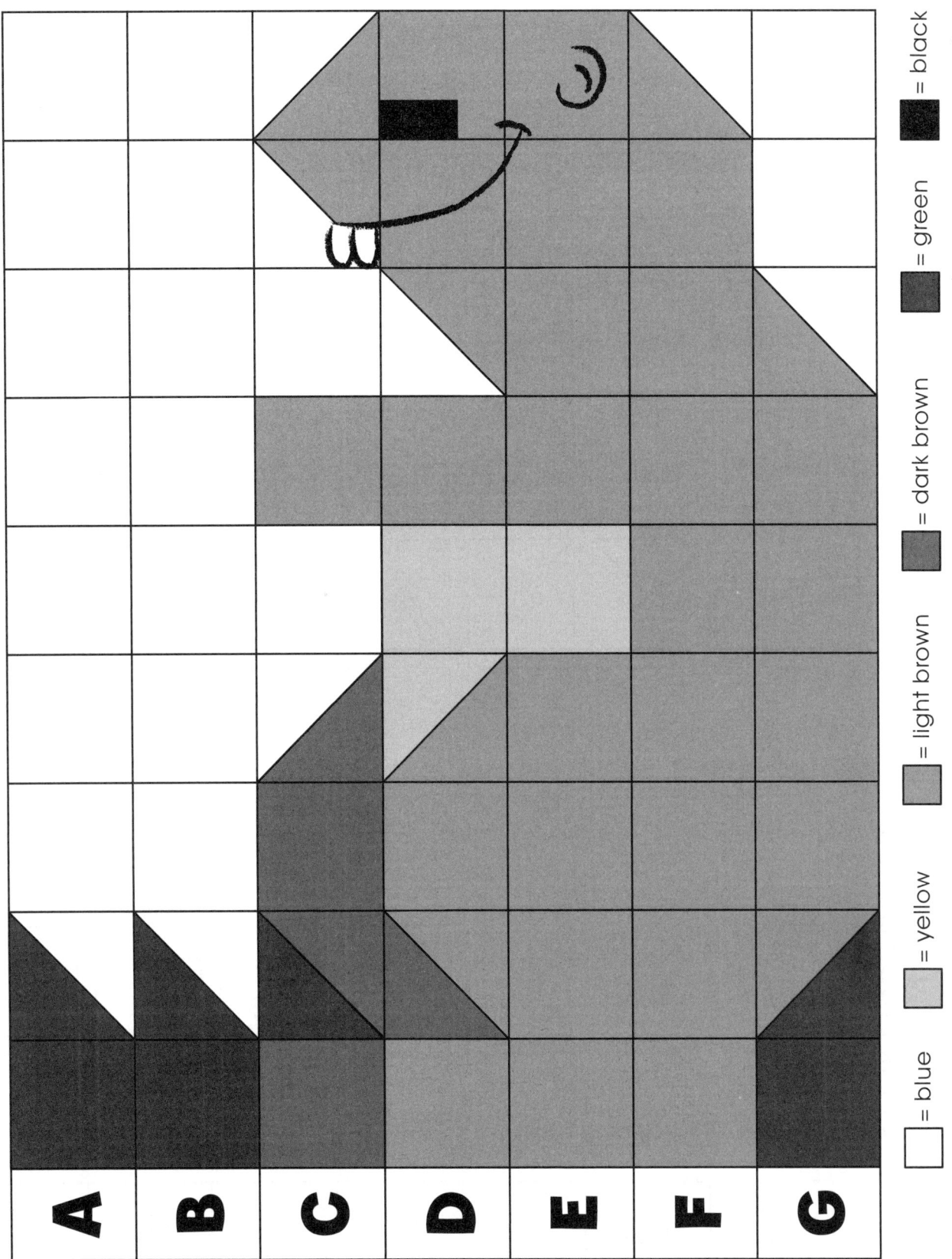

Hidden Picture 21

Directions: Use the information below to color each square on the separate sheet of blank graph paper.

	A	B	C	D	E	F	G
9	purple	purple	purple	purple	purple	purple	purple
8	purple	pink	pink	pink/red	red/pink	pink	purple
7	purple	pink	pink	pink/red	red	red/pink	purple
6	purple	pink	pink	pink/red	red	red/pink	purple
5	purple	pink/red	red/pink	pink/red	red/pink	pink	purple
4	purple	pink/red	red	red/pink	pink	pink	purple
3	purple	pink/red	red	red/pink	pink	pink	purple
2	purple	pink/red	red/pink	pink	pink	pink	purple
1	purple	purple	purple	purple	purple	purple	purple

Hidden Picture 21

Answer Key: Valentine Hearts

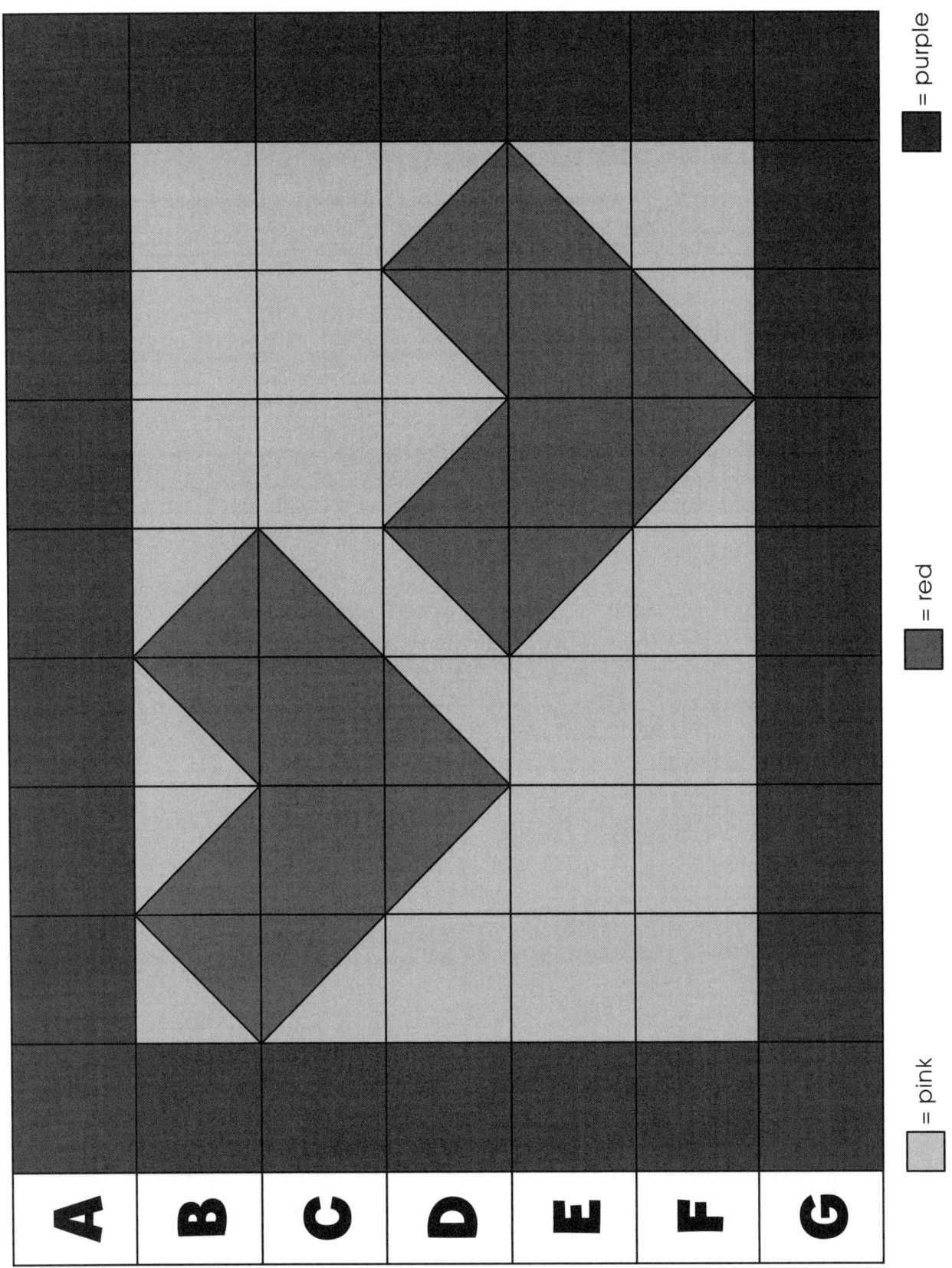

Hidden Picture 22 — Directions

Directions: Use the information below to color each square on the separate sheet of blank graph paper.

	A	B	C	D	E	F	G
1	light blue	light blue	light blue	light blue	light blue	light blue	light blue
2	light blue	green	green	green	green	green	light blue
3	light blue	green	green	green	green	green	light blue
4	light blue	green	green	green	green	green	light blue
5	light blue	green	green/yellow	yellow	yellow/green	green	light blue
6	light blue	black	yellow	black	yellow	black	light blue
7	light blue	black	yellow	black	yellow	black	light blue
8	light blue	green	green/yellow	yellow	yellow/green	green	light blue
9	green	green	green	green	green	green	green

Hidden Picture 22

Answer Key: Leprechaun Hat

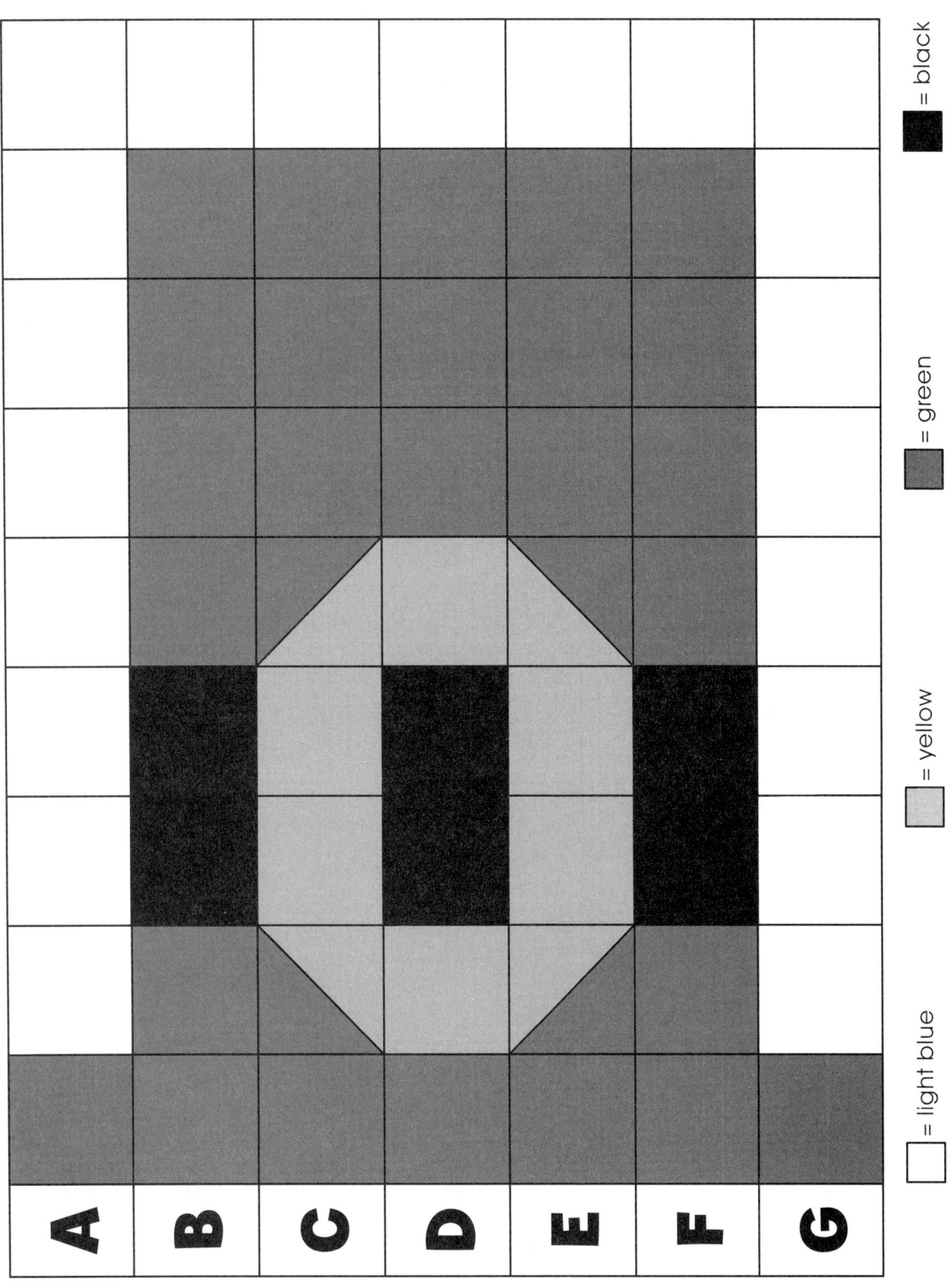

Hidden Picture 23 — Directions

Directions: Use the information below to color each square on the separate sheet of blank graph paper. Draw a nose. Draw a mouth. Draw whiskers.

	A	B	C	D	E	F	G
1	blue	blue	white	blue / yellow	yellow	yellow / green	green
2	blue	blue	blue	yellow	yellow	yellow	yellow
3	blue	blue	blue	yellow	yellow	yellow	yellow
4	yellow / pink	pink / yellow / blue	blue	blue / yellow	yellow	yellow	green / yellow
5	blue / yellow / pink	pink / yellow	blue / yellow	yellow	yellow	yellow	yellow
6	blue	blue / yellow	yellow	black / yellow	yellow	yellow	green / yellow
7	blue	blue / yellow	yellow	black / yellow	yellow	yellow	yellow
8	blue / yellow / pink	pink / yellow	blue / yellow	yellow	yellow / blue	blue / green	green / yellow
9	yellow / pink	pink / yellow / blue	blue	blue	blue	blue / green	green

Hidden Picture 23

Answer Key: Easter Bunny

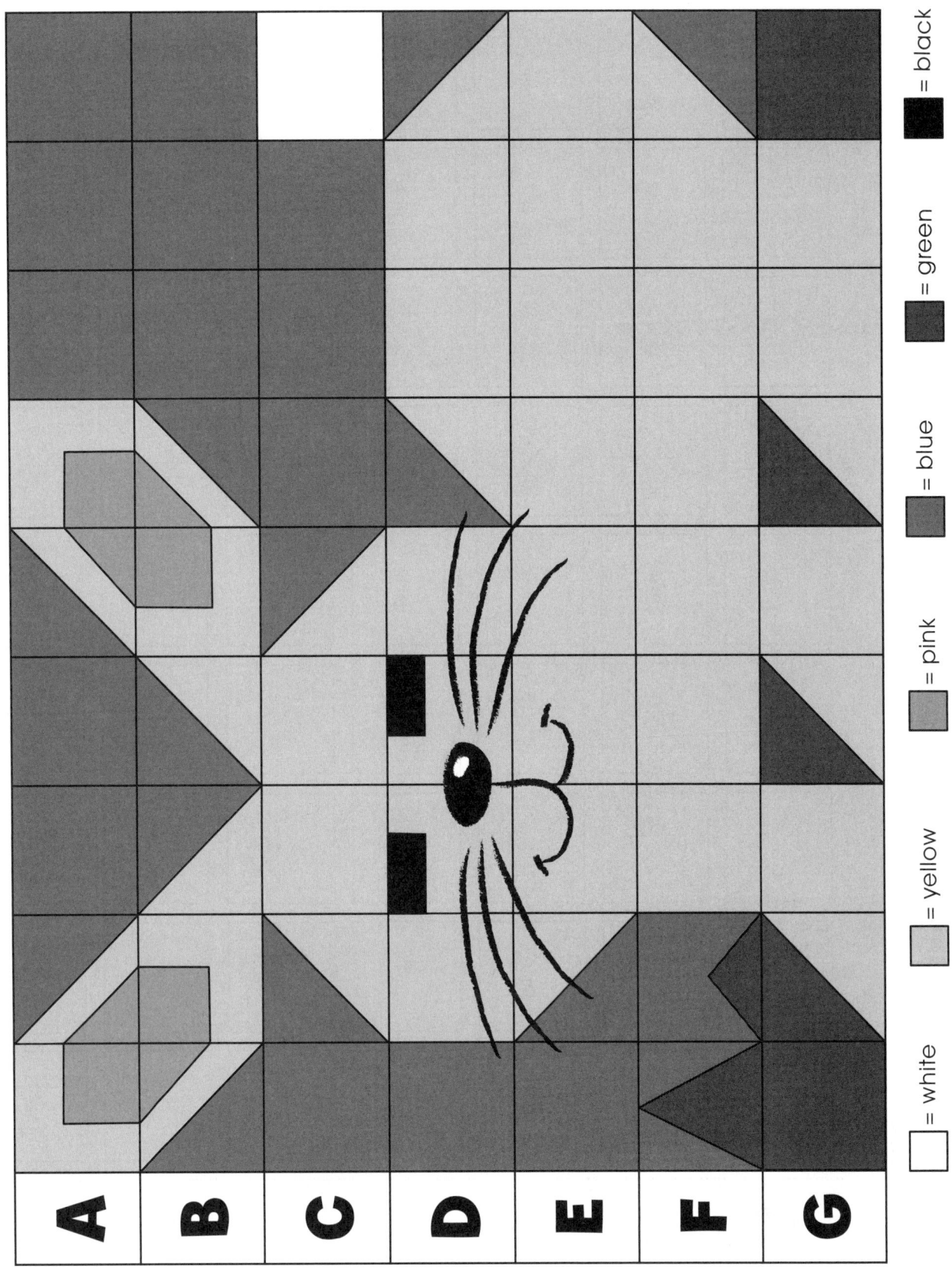

Hidden Picture 24 — Directions

Directions: Use the information below to color each square on the separate sheet of blank graph paper.

	A	B	C	D	E	F	G
7	green	green/pink	pink	pink	pink	pink/green	green
6	green/pink	pink	pink	pink	pink	pink	pink/green
5	yellow/pink	pink/yellow	yellow/pink	pink/yellow	yellow/pink	pink/yellow	yellow/pink
4	pink/yellow	yellow/pink	pink/yellow	yellow/pink	pink/yellow	yellow/pink	pink/yellow
3	pink	pink	pink	pink	pink	pink	pink
2	yellow/pink	pink/yellow	yellow/pink	pink/yellow	yellow/pink	pink/yellow	yellow/pink
1	pink/yellow	yellow/pink	pink/yellow	yellow/pink	pink/yellow	yellow/pink	pink/yellow
0	green/pink	pink	pink	pink	pink	pink	pink/green
-1	green	green/pink	pink	pink	pink	pink/green	green

© Carson-Dellosa • CD-104282

Early Graphing Hidden Pictures

Hidden Picture 24

Answer Key: Easter Egg

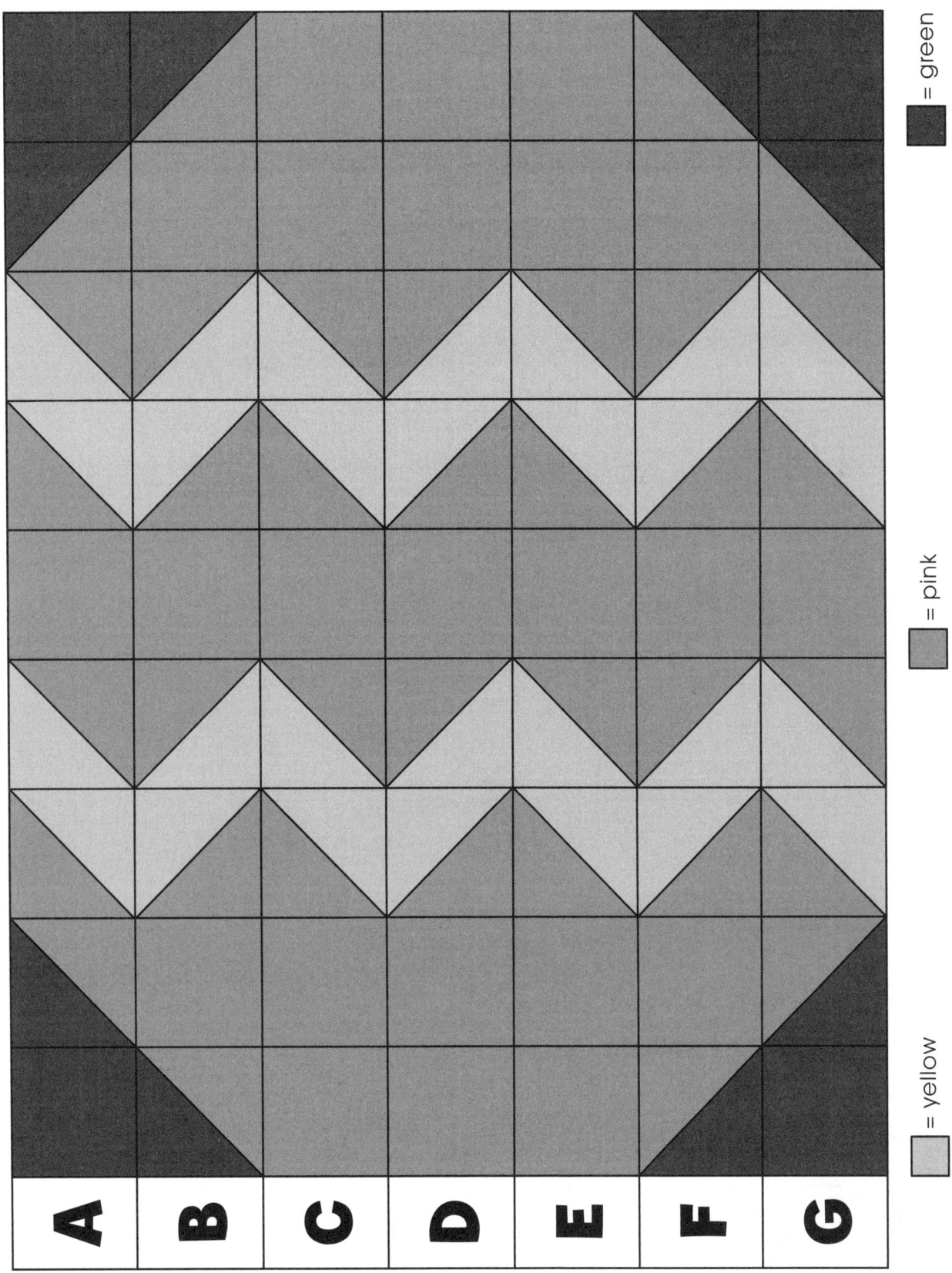

Hidden Picture 25 — Directions

Directions: Use the information below to color each square on the separate sheet of blank graph paper.

	A	B	C	D	E	F	G
1	green	green	green	green	green	green	green
2	green	green/orange	orange	orange	orange	orange	orange/green
3	green	orange	orange/yellow	orange	orange/yellow	yellow/orange	orange
4	green	orange	orange/yellow	orange	orange	yellow	orange
5	brown/green	orange	orange	orange/yellow	orange	yellow	orange
6	green/brown	orange	orange	orange/yellow	orange	yellow	orange
7	green	orange	orange/yellow	orange	orange	yellow	orange
8	green	orange	orange/yellow	orange	orange/yellow	yellow/orange	orange
9	green	green/orange	orange	orange	orange	orange	orange/green

Hidden Picture 25   Answer Key: Jack-O'-Lantern

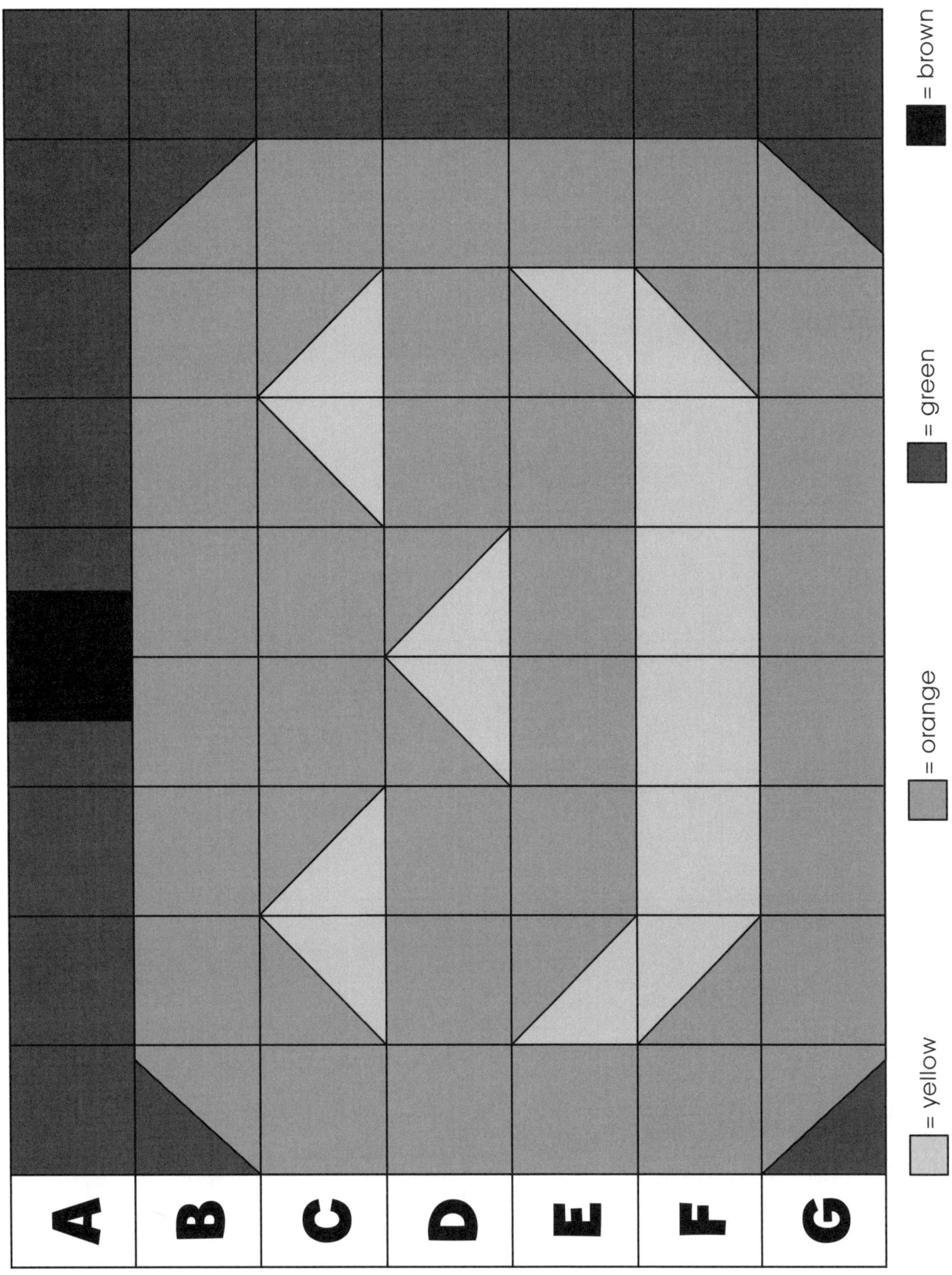

Hidden Picture 26 — Directions

Directions: Use the information below to color each square on the separate sheet of blank graph paper. Draw a face. Draw ears.

	A	B	C	D	E	F	G
Row 1	yellow	yellow	yellow/black	black/yellow	yellow	yellow	yellow
Row 2	yellow	yellow/black	black	black	black/yellow	yellow	yellow
Row 3	yellow	yellow/black	black	black	black	black/yellow	yellow
Row 4	yellow	yellow	yellow/black	black	black	yellow	yellow
Row 5	yellow	yellow	gray	gray	gray	gray/yellow	yellow
Row 6	yellow	yellow	yellow/black	black	black	yellow	yellow
Row 7	yellow	yellow/black	black	black	black	black/yellow	yellow
Row 8	yellow	yellow/black	black	black	black/yellow	yellow	yellow
Row 9	yellow	yellow	yellow/black	black/yellow	yellow	yellow	yellow

Hidden Picture 26

Answer Key: Bat

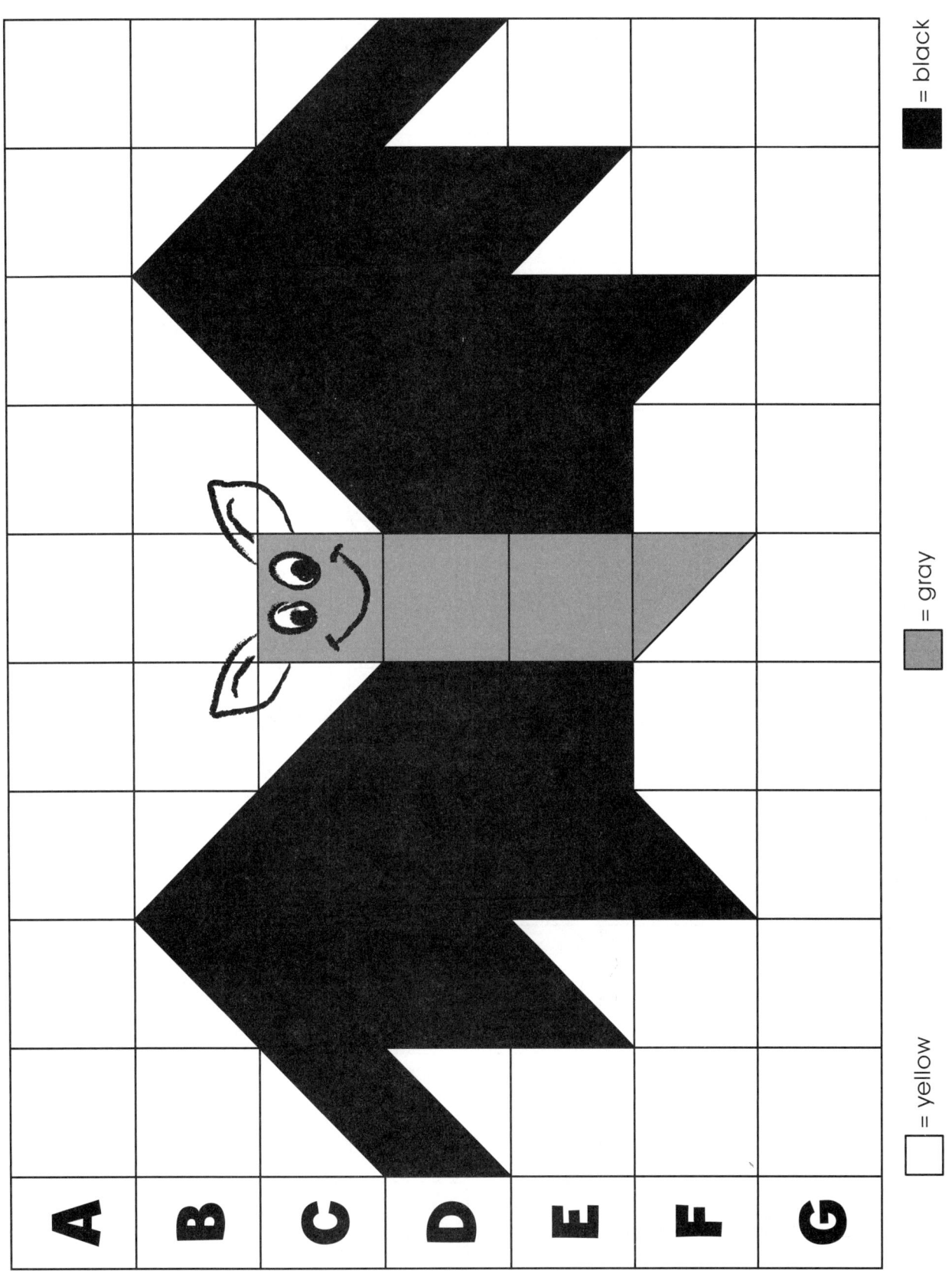

Hidden Picture 27

Directions: Use the information below to color each square on the separate sheet of blank graph paper. Draw eyes.

	A	B	C	D	E	F	G
9	blue	blue	blue	blue	blue	blue	green
8	blue	orange	orange / blue	blue	blue / red	red / blue	green
7	blue	blue / orange	orange	orange / blue	red / dark brown	dark brown / red	green / orange
6	blue / red	red	red / light brown	light brown / orange	dark brown	dark brown	orange
5	blue / orange	orange	light brown	light brown	orange / dark brown	dark brown / red	green
4	blue / orange	orange	light brown	light brown	orange / dark brown	dark brown / red	green
3	blue / red	red	red / light brown	light brown / orange	dark brown	dark brown	orange
2	blue	blue / orange	orange	orange / blue	red / dark brown	dark brown / red	green / orange
1	blue	orange	orange / blue	blue	blue / red	red / blue	green

Hidden Picture 27 **Answer Key: Turkey**

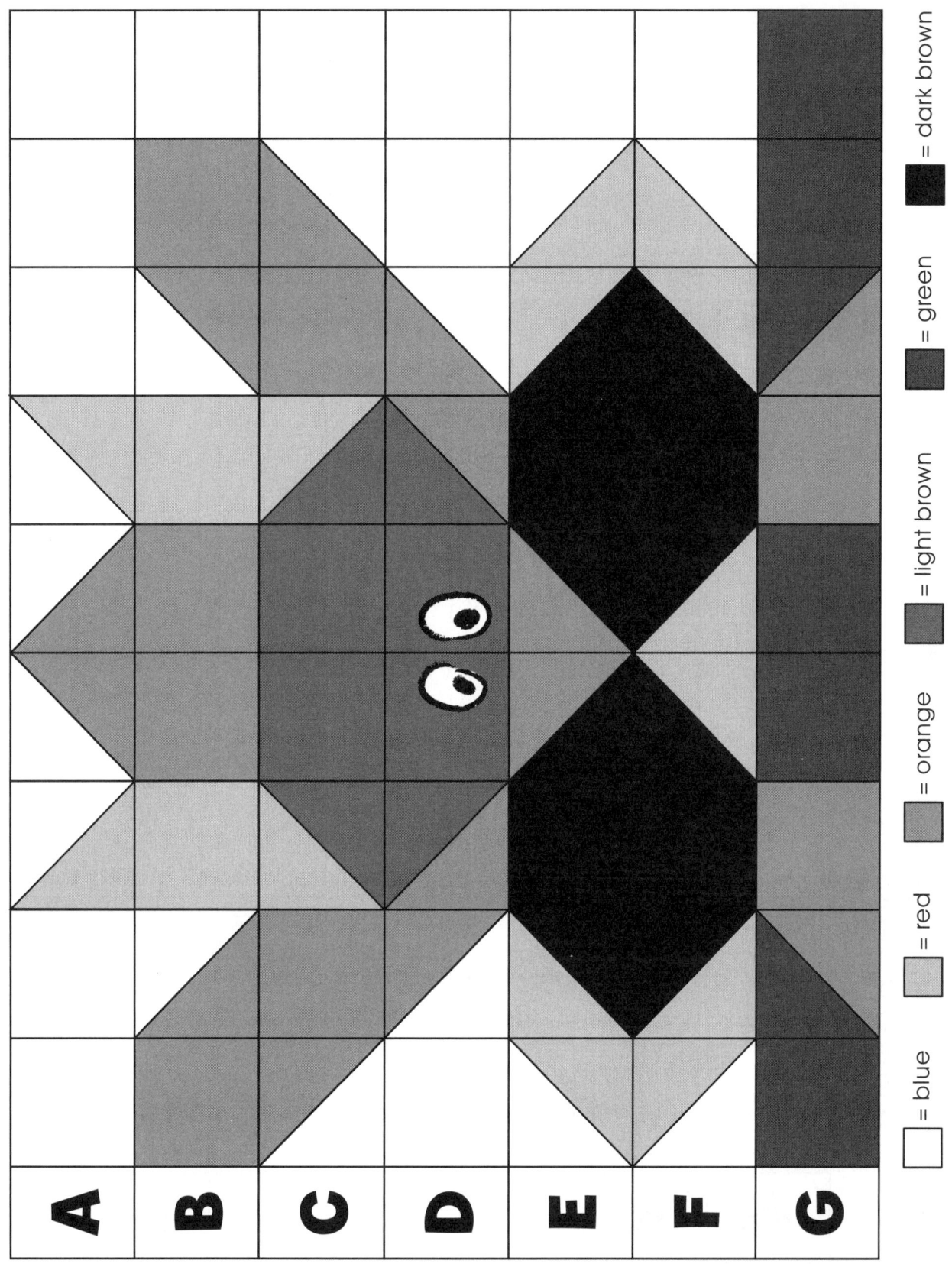

© Carson-Dellosa • CD-104282   Early Graphing Hidden Pictures

Hidden Picture 28 — Directions

Directions: Use the information below to color each square on the separate sheet of blank graph paper.

	A	B	C	D	E	F	G
9	blue	blue	blue/yellow	yellow/blue	blue	blue	blue
8	blue	blue	blue/yellow	yellow/blue	blue	blue	blue
7	blue	blue	white	white	blue	blue	blue
6	blue	blue	white	white	blue	blue	blue
5	blue	blue	white	white	blue	blue	blue
4	blue	blue	white	white	blue	green	green
3	green	green	white	white	green	green	green
2	green	green	green/red	red/green	green	green	blue
1	brown	green	green/red	red/green	green	brown	brown

© Carson-Dellosa • CD-104282   58   Early Graphing Hidden Pictures

Hidden Picture 28 **Answer Key: Holiday Candle**

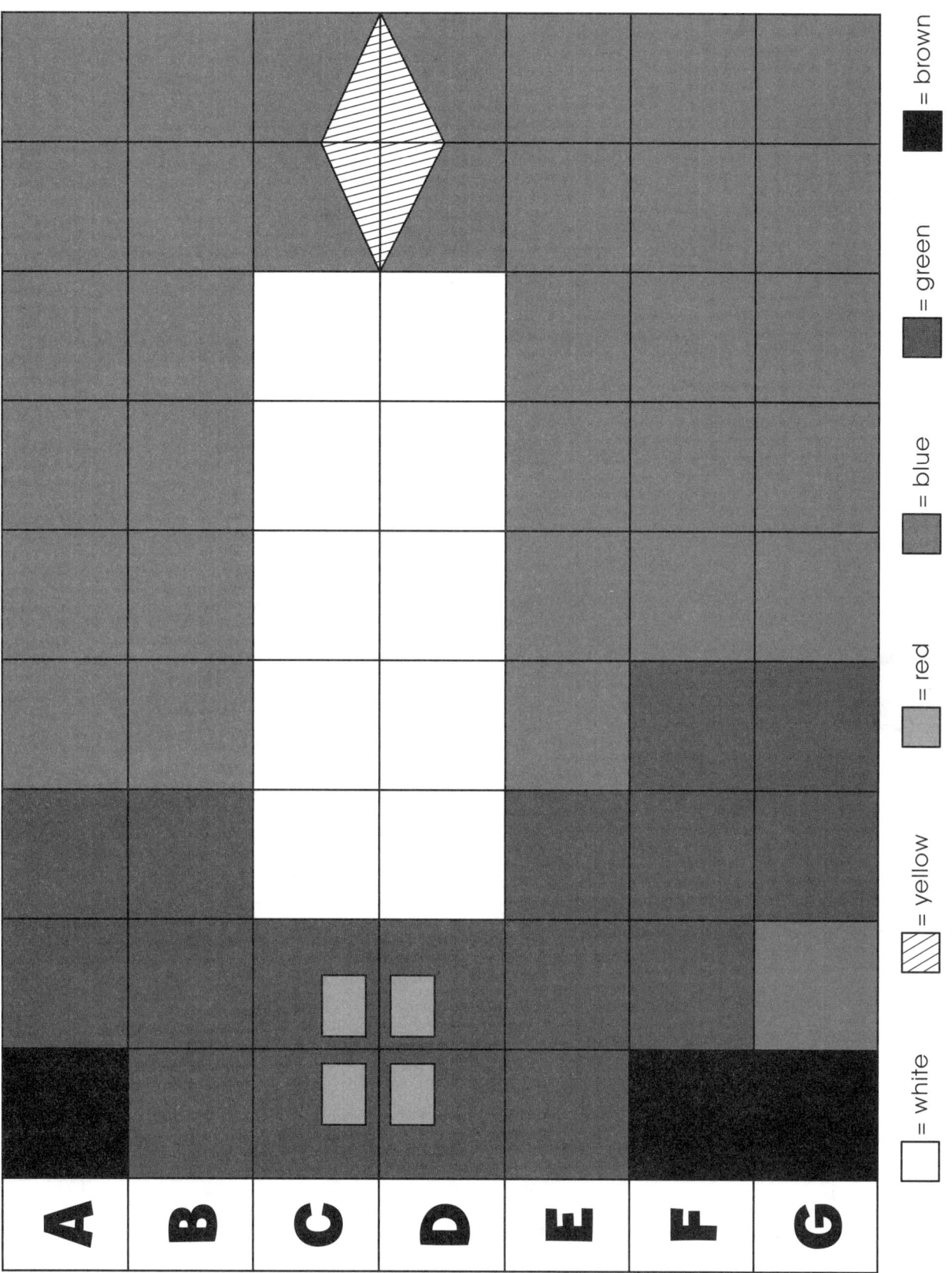

Hidden Picture 29 — Directions

Directions: Use the information below to color each square on the separate sheet of blank graph paper.

	A	B	C	D	E	F	G
1	blue	blue	blue	blue	blue	blue	blue
2	blue	blue/white	red	white/blue	blue	blue	blue
3	blue	red	blue	white/red	blue	blue	blue
4	blue	blue	blue	red/white	blue	blue	blue
5	blue	blue	green/blue	white/red	blue/green	blue	blue
6	blue	blue	green	green	green	blue	blue
7	blue	blue	green/blue	white/red	blue/green	blue	blue
8	blue	blue	blue	red/white	blue	blue	blue
9	blue	blue	blue	white/red	blue	blue	blue

© Carson-Dellosa • CD-104282 — Early Graphing Hidden Pictures

Hidden Picture 29

Answer Key: Candy Cane

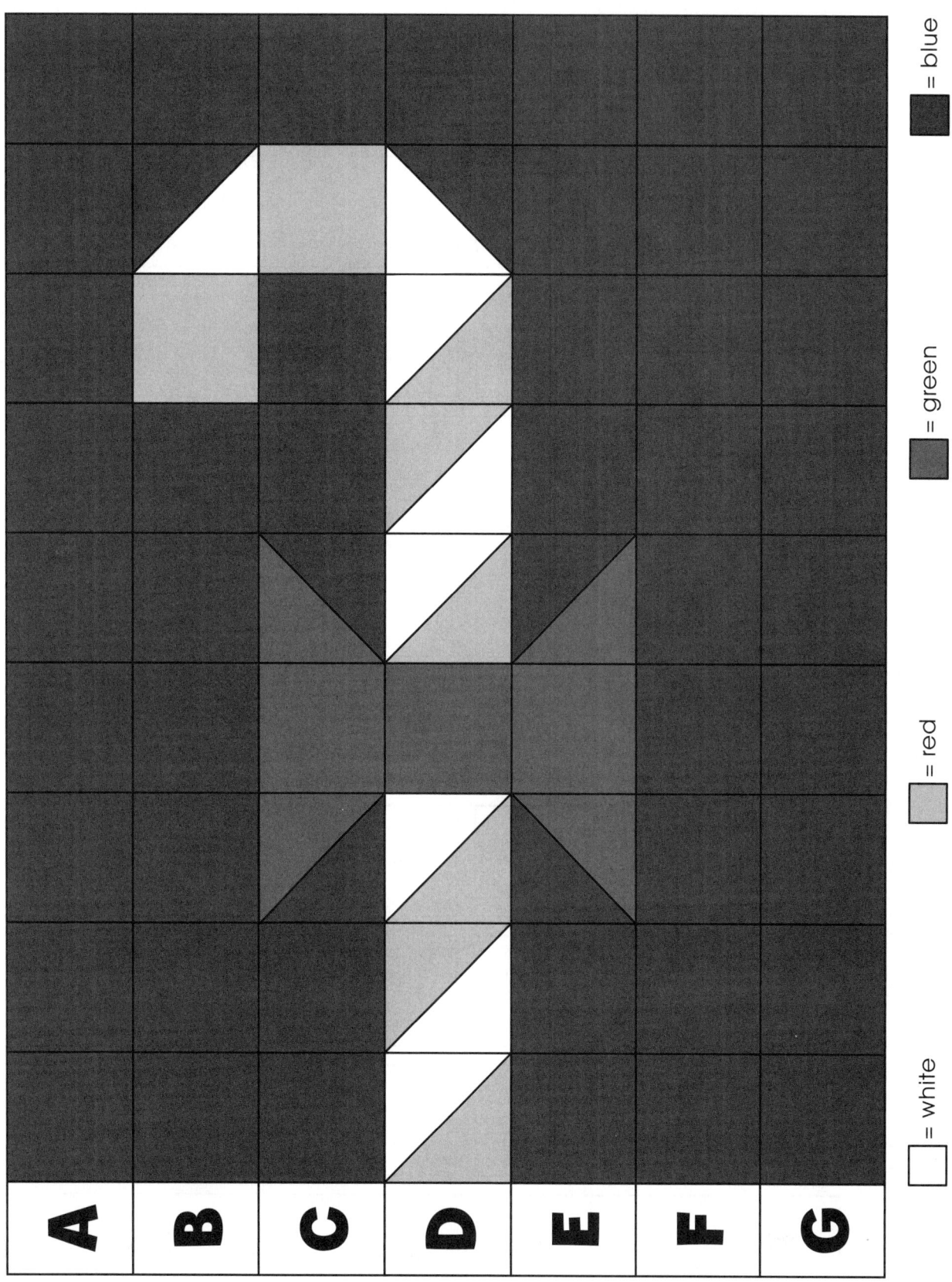

Hidden Picture 30

Directions: Use the information below to color each square on the separate sheet of blank graph paper.

	A	B	C	D	E	F	G
9	green	green	green	green	green	green	green
8	green	green	white	white	white	white	white/green
7	green	green	white	white	white	white	white/green
6	green	green	green/red	red	red	red	green
5	green	green	green/red	red	red	red	green
4	green	green	green/red	red	red	red	green
3	green	green/red	red	red	red	red	green
2	green	red	red	red	red	red	green
1	green	green/red	red	red	red	red/green	green

Hidden Picture 30

Answer Key: Christmas Stocking

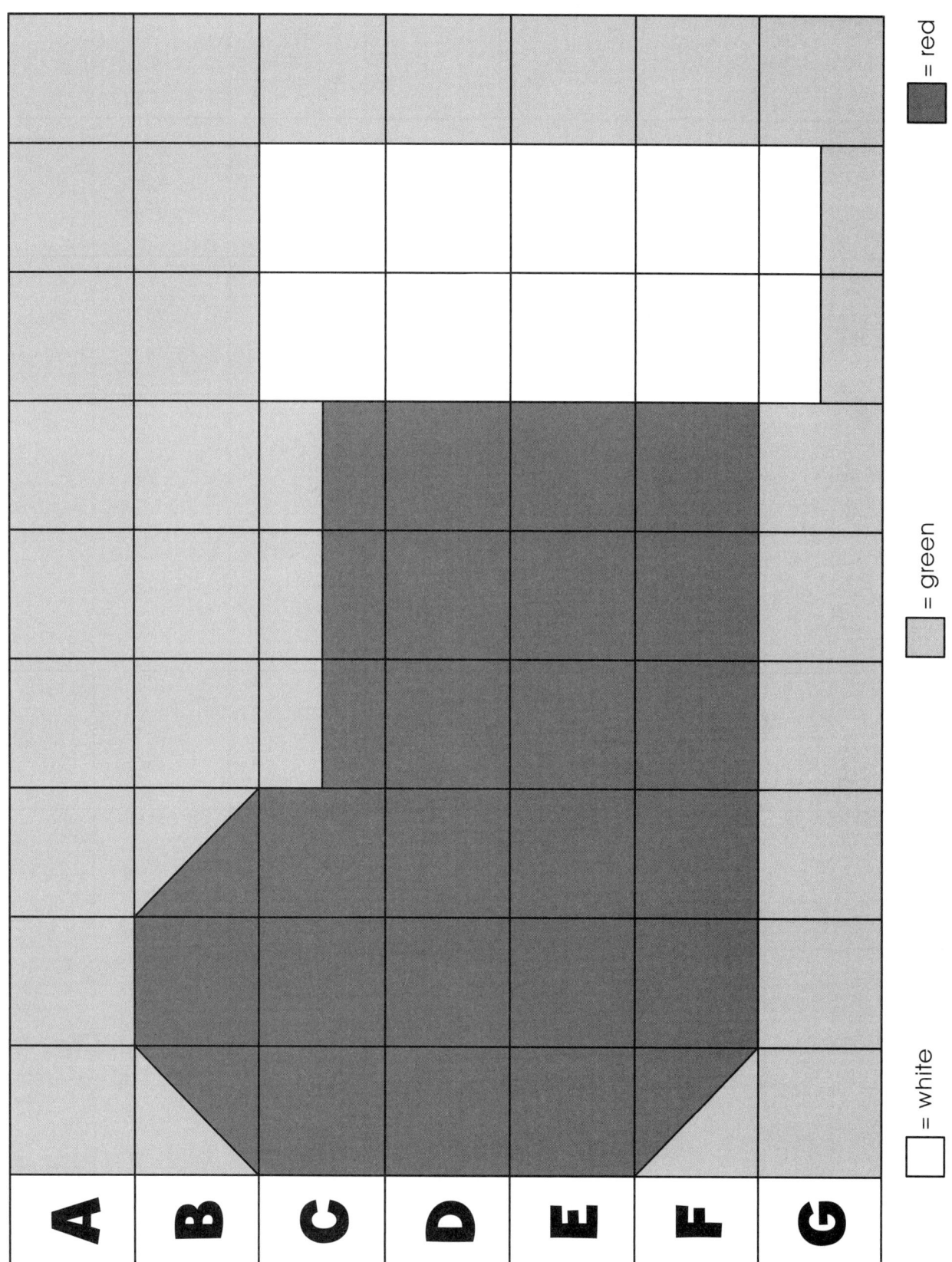

Name: _____

Hidden Picture: _____

| A | B | C | D | E | F | G |